(Department of Accounting, College of Administration and Economics/ University of I
hisham noori hussain AL-hashimy   978-1-62265-912-8 (online) 978-1-62265-913-

I0051239

Introduction to management skills must be available to accountants in Iraq

Hisham Noori Hussain

Published by IISTE Book Publishing in the United States

978-1-62265-912-8 (online) 978-1-62265-913-5 (paper)

(Department of Accounting, College of Administration and Economics/ University of Basra, Iraq)
hisham noori hussain AL-hashimy   978-1-62265-912-8 (online) 978-1-62265-913-5 (paper)

Introduction to management skills must be available to accountants in

Iraq

(Department of Accounting, College of Administration and Economics/ University of Basra, Iraq)
hisham noori hussain AL-hashimy   978-1-62265-912-8 (online) 978-1-62265-913-5 (paper)

(Department of Accounting, College of Administration and Economics/ University of Basra, Iraq)
hisham noori hussain AL-hashimy   978-1-62265-912-8 (online) 978-1-62265-913-5 (paper)

Introduction to management skills must be available to accountants in Iraq

Hisham Noori Hussain

(Department of Accounting, College of Administration and Economics/ University of Basra, Iraq)
hisham noori hussain AL-hashimy   978-1-62265-912-8 (online) 978-1-62265-913-5 (paper)

Dedication

I dedicate this book first to my wonderful family, my first teacher my dear father, my dear mother and my distinguished brother. I also dedicate this book to my fellow faculty members at Al-Basra University accounting department I hope this book will be a simple addition to the global community.

Hisham noori hussain

(Department of Accounting, College of Administration and Economics/ University of Basra, Iraq)
hisham noori hussain AL-hashimy   978-1-62265-912-8 (online) 978-1-62265-913-5 (paper)

ABOUT THE AUTHORS

Author Hisham Noori Hussain Al-Hashimy is a member of the faculty of Basra University. He holds a master's degree in accounting from the University of Infrastructure in Malaysia and has published many researches like (A Review of Creative Accounting Practices and Its Area, Technique and Ways of Prevention),(Factor Influencing Salaries and Wage Order: Empirical Study at Basra University), (A Review and Model Development of the Factors that Affect Mobile Marketing Acceptance by Customers) ,(A Review of the Factors that Influence the Adoption of Cloud Computing by Small and Medium Enterprises) And others. Also it received many international certificates in economics and statistics computer skills, English and International Accounting.

(Department of Accounting, College of Administration and Economics/ University of Basra, Iraq)
hisham noori hussain AL-hashimy   978-1-62265-912-8 (online) 978-1-62265-913-5 (paper)

PREFACE

This book contains all the managerial skills that accountants must be aware of in order to become a successful accountant and administrator. This book provides all the problems facing employees and managers and how to address them through the separation of organizational behavior and human resources. The book includes all legal issues and information that must be available in the accountant to be successful and there is very important legal information is necessary for the accountant to be aware of them. The book contains information about manipulating accounts and how to deal with them, as well as very important economic treatments. Managers face many of the administrative and legal problems, and these problems should be resolved either in the short term or in the long term. This book presents most of the obstacles faced by managers and how to address them. Accountants must be aware of the administrative problems they face in professional life in order to address them and are characterized in a simple and simple way, thus not delaying the work of organizations.

(Department of Accounting, College of Administration and Economics/ University of Basra, Iraq)
hisham noori hussain AL-hashimy   978-1-62265-912-8 (online) 978-1-62265-913-5 (paper)

Contents

(Department of Accounting, College of Administration and Economics/ University of Basra, Iraq)
hisham noori hussain AL-hashimy   978-1-62265-912-8 (online) 978-1-62265-913-5 (paper)

(Department of Accounting, College of Administration and Economics/ University of Basra, Iraq)
hisham noori hussain AL-hashimy   978-1-62265-912-8 (online) 978-1-62265-913-5 (paper)

CHAPTER 1

Organization behavior and human resource

Invisible barrier, <u>which is observed to prevent women and minorities from achieving the highest positions in the organizations?</u>

The glass ceiling, which was a phrase coined in the 1980s, is a representation of the invisible and artificial barriers that block women and minorities from advancing up the corporate ladder to management and executive positions.

<u>Based on the above, what are the causes?</u>

The glass ceiling effect is caused by several factors such as:

Job segregation

Most women and minorities who are professionals are not given the opportunity to lead in an organization. Many are given posts as staff and supporting jobs compared to the men who are usually given opportunities to lead in a business path where they would have more chances to be promoted to higher positions

Perception

One of the most important barriers to women's career advancement would be the colleagues and managers' perception who see them as less committed and are not able to balance their domestic and professional responsibilities.

Gender stereotyping

Male superiors tend to choose individuals like them to lead the organization as most organizations are male dominated. Gender discrimination is employers' bias or unfair attitudes toward women in managerial selection, placement, training and promotion opportunities. Gender discrimination refers to how individuals are treated differently because of their gender. In this case, such gender discrimination usually involves women.

<u>Based on the question above, how to overcome such barrier?</u>

10

Equality in education is an important issue, as gender equality guidelines improve education for both men and women. The goal of providing better education for women does not mean neglecting or suppressing men. By placing men and women on an equal level, the relatively increased valuing of women will also benefit men by informing them of the strengths, capabilities and contributions of members of the opposite sex. It may also decrease the pressure many males conform to the traditional roles, behaviors and ways of thinking.

The differences among countries affect HR planning at organizations with international operations

The most common difficulties in effective HR management are cross-cultural adaptation, different organizational/workforce values, and differences in management, management style and turnover. Doing business globally requires that adaptations be made to reflect these factors. It is crucial that such concerns be seen as interrelated by managers and professionals as they do business and establish operations globally.

The nature and stability of political systems vary from country to country. U.S. firms are accustomed to a relatively stable political system, and the same is true in many of the other developed countries in Europe. Although presidents, prime ministers, premiers, governors, senators, and representatives may change, the legal systems are well-established, and global firms can depend on continuity and consistency. However, in many other nations, the legal and political systems are turbulent. Some governments regularly are overthrown by military coups. Others are ruled by dictators and despots who use their power to require international firms to buy goods and services from host-country firms owned or controlled by the rulers or the rulers' families.

International firms may have to decide strategically when to comply with certain laws and regulations and when to ignore them because of operational or political reasons. Another issue involves ethics. Because of restrictions imposed on you. S. -based firms through the Foreign Corrupt Practices Act

(FCPA), a fine line exists between paying "agent fees," which is legal, and bribery, which is illegal.HR regulations and laws vary among countries in character and detail. In many Western European countries, laws on labor unions and employment make it difficult to reduce the number of workers because required payments to former employees can be very high, as the HR Perspective on the next page indicates. Equal employment legislation exists in varying degrees.

Economic factors affect the other three factors. Different countries have different economic systems. Some even still operate with a modified version of communism, which has essentially failed. For example, in China communism is the official economic approach. But as the government attempts to move to a more mixed model, it is using unemployment and layoffs to reduce government enterprises bloated with too many workers. Political instability can lead to situations in which the assets of foreign firms are seized. In addition, nations with weak economies may not be able to invest in maintaining and upgrading the necessary elements of their infrastructures, such as roads, electric power, schools, and telecommunications. The absence of good infrastructures may make it more difficult to convince managers from the United States or Japan to take assignments overseas.

What would persuade an employee to take a foreign assignment give appropriate examples?

Employers can persuade employees by making several offers to entice employees into accepting foreign assignments. Employers can offer repatriation assistance plus a guarantee they can come back to their former role post assignment. As most employees that need to be convinced of taking such a step are those in the upper hierarchy of the organisation, they need to be convinced that the company is willing to provide job security should something go wrong.

Other than that, an offer to cover a number of round trip airfares to return for family visits could also help persuade an employee as family care and approval is one of the most important factors in rejecting foreign assignments. For example, an employee in Malaysia, being offered a foreign assignment in China, may reject the assignment as he is not ready to part with his immediate family. Thus, such an offer could reassure him of ample opportunities to see his family.

An employee could perhaps be convinced to take up the foreign assignment if he is given the opportunity to visit the foreign country prior to accepting the assignment. A paid trip to visit the country as an offer could help persuade a reluctant employee.

In cases where the foreign country speaks a different language, the employers could assist in providing the relevant language training course beforehand. Many employees fear that miscommunication may occur when working in foreign countries, resulting in disastrous consequences. An example of this is of someone in Malaysia being reassigned to France, but does not speak a word of French. Miscommunication could have him or her deported immediately, and many employees fear such instances.

Lastly, immigration assistance for your spouse in order that they could obtain employment could help ease persuasion, as employees find it easier adapting to new environments when they have someone dear to them close by.

Self-management leadership is defined as the process of leading others to lead themselves. Why self-management leadership failed to function effectively.

Self-management is the process of empowering an individual with the minimum knowledge and skills needed in a certain area until the person can recycle that knowledge and skills and so improve on it over time until he exercises self-leadership in that particular area. However, there are some disadvantages that cause self-management fail to function effectively.

The first is that a self-managed person can, for instance, set an unrealistically high expectation or goal. If the goal cannot be achieved, the person may become frustrated. This kind of dysfunctional self-controlling behavior can be unproductive. To avoid this problem, it is important from time-to-time for people to discuss their goals first with someone else before going about fulfilling those goals on their own.

Then there is the situation that if a person becomes too self-managed, they may have trouble listening to higher level management to ensure the big picture is properly understood and the results of his/her work is relevant to the needs of the organization.

There are people who are well-trained in the traditional and competitive management style. These people are more likely to aggressively compete and use peer pressure to disrupt the self-management system and so make it become dysfunctional. It is therefore important for the team's overall authority to intervene and correct the problem.

How employees evaluate the fairness of a pay structure based on Equity Theory.

Equity theory focuses on two sides: the input and the outcome. An employee compares his or her job's inputs with an outcomes ratio. If the employee perceives inequality, he or she he will act to correct the inequity. The employee may lower productivity or reduce the quality of their job. Many times inequities can lead to an increase in absenteeism and even resignation of an organization. Equity theory deals with human motives and it should

14

have wide applications in understanding organizational behavior. HRD needs to take equity theory under serious consideration when dealing with people whether in cases of administering simple tasks like pay, promotions, and recognition or in cases of training, improvements, and development. Equity theory will help HRD explain employee's behavior and provide them with the possible factors that might decrease efficiency and performance.

The fairness of exchange between employees and employer is not usually perceived by the employees as simply as an economic matter, an element of relative justice is involved. Equity theory could be applied to any social situation in which an exchange takes place (e.g., between a man and his wife, between football team mates, and between employee and his employer). When two people exchange something, there is a possibility that one or both will feel that the exchange was inequitable. This is the case frequently when an individual exchanges his services for pay.

In the past, it was found that a large share of expatriate managers from the United States had returned home before successfully completing their foreign assignments. Suggest 2 way possible reasons for the high failure rate.

Expatriate failure is usually defined as a posting that either ends prematurely or is considered ineffective by senior management. Most research into the matter has come to the conclusion that failure rates are high and can vary between 20% and 50% depending on the country.

The costs of failure have been estimated by numerous means with widely varying results. Despite the lack of clarity, it is clear that a failed assignment in an overseas location is considerably more expensive than one occurring closer to home. Below are the chief factors resulting in an unsuccessful expatriate assignment?

The first possible reason for the failure is family stress. Most expatriate managers are challenged and excited to be in their new postings. They need to spend a lot of time at work since they are under pressure to adapt to the new culture and their overall responsibilities are often larger than they have

15

experienced before. This may affect their relationship with their spouses and family.

The responsibility overload is also one of the reasons. In almost all cases, the responsibilities of expatriates in developing countries will be larger than they are used to overseeing. Given the nature of emerging countries in Southeast Asia, expatriates may supervise 5 to 10 times more people than ever before.

Types of employees

Employee Merit Pay

Employee merit pay can be defined as a system of linking pay increases to rating on performance appraisal. Rather than paying all staff the exact same pay, this system is actually paying more to better performers due to the fact that they contributed to the company performance. Thus, in a fairness point of view, the staff should be rewarded with better pay scheme. In addition, such merit pay system is also encourages the staff to continue strive for better performance in order to get higher pay. In organization point of view, the dimension of measurement can be designed in a way ties back to company desired behavior on staff. If a staff is working to fulfill the dimension, the staff is fulfilling the organization goals as well. Such a merit pay system has been implemented in most of the company in the world. For example, Merck which is the giant drug company is using such system to reward the performers. The have two main factors which is the individual performance rating and individual pay ratio to average pay. Staff who performer better in Key Performance Index (KPI) will be given higher score. The score will eventually be translated into the pay scheme calculation from 0%, 50%, 100%, 150% or even 200% pay increase to the staff. Such merit system is able to reward high pay to best performers and distinguish them from the low performers. The best performers could earn up to two times as compared to the lowest performers in the company.

(Department of Accounting, College of Administration and Economics/ University of Basra, Iraq)
hisham noori hussain AL-hashimy   978-1-62265-912-8 (online) 978-1-62265-913-5 (paper)

Employee Discipline

Employee discipline is a broad word which comprise of a broad scope. The word "discipline" means to follow the rules, laws and procedures in an organization or social unit. In addition, it can be related to instruction, learning, and improvement. On the other hand, "discipline" can be also mean for correction and punishment. The employee is the person which employed by the organization itself. However, applying discipline does not necessary produce effective discipline staff. There are some objectives behind the employee discipline which includes compliance and conformance to rules, correction of behavior that violated the rules, re-asserting authority, and punishing the wrong-doing. The discipline is actually been stated in the letter of offer on the job or even contract of employment. For example, the standard clause that will appear in the standard employment contracts are like failing to attend to work, cheating on the claim and report, office harassment and others. Any staff that violated such clauses should be handled using standard disciplinary action such as warning letters, followed by domestic enquiry, corrective actions monitoring and finally removal of the staff is the behavior is not improving.

Employee Benefit

Employee benefits are all forms of consideration given by an entity, an organization in exchange for service provided by employees. In other word, employee benefits are any form of return back to employees in terms of monetary, recognition and others. Different company and industry will have different employee benefits. For example, manufacturing industry will have higher insurance coverage; financial industry will have higher number of paid annual leave. Employee benefit can be categorized as short-term employee benefits, post-employment benefits, long-term benefits, benefits for employment termination contract and compensation in equity. For example, short-term benefits are allowance, EPF contributions, paid annual leave, paid medical leave, bonuses, medical care, car loan, medical check-up subsidization. Post-employment benefits are including retirement life insurance, medical care. Benefit for employment contract termination as including the Voluntary Separation Scheme (VSS) with numbers of salary month paid. Compensation in form of equity participations are like Employee Share Ownership Scheme (ESOS).

Employee development

Employee development is to develop the abilities of an individual employee in terms of competencies, skills, knowledge, career path and others. The idea of employee development is not only on individual skill, but also the overall employee growth in terms of career, position, job scope, job enlargement and empowerment. This is directly related to the growth of the company in terms of performance, succession plan and talent management of the company. Employee development is a key to employee motivation as employee is motivated with development plan that arranged for them. Employee with high motivation is always one of the important people agenda for Human Resource department as high motivation staff leads to high performance, in which translated into company performance. There are several examples of employee development activities such as coaching where experience, skills, and knowledge will be shared from more experience senior. Secondly, training program which focusing on technical skill, communication skill and other soft skills can be arranged. Thirdly is about empowerment where a staff is given a bigger authority and job responsibility to train up the management skills. Finally, it is about promotion and delegation where it involves the actual career recognition and scope of authority.

Human resource careers

Human resource careers could include hundreds of careers depending on the size of the company, its operations, and the industry that the company is working. The following only discusses six of the most important careers in human resources. In this article, six careers of human resources are discussed. The most important two careers are utilized at the end of the articles.

1- Human Resources Officer

In any company, the responsibilities of human resources (HR) officer is developing, advising on, and implementing policies that are relate to the effective use of employees within an company. The aim of HR officer is to ensure that the organization employs the right balance of staff in terms of skills and experience, and that training and development opportunities are available to employees to enhance their performance and achieve the employer's business aims. HR officers are involved in a range of activities required by organizations, regardless of the size or type of business. These cover areas such as: (1) working practices; (2) recruitment; (3) pay; (4) conditions of employment; (5) negotiation with external work-related agencies; (6) equality and diversity.

Typical HR officer responsibility might include the following:
Work with other departments, providing consultancy, providing assistance to the line managers to understand and implement policies and procedures;
Promote equality and diversity as part of the culture of the organization;
Liaise with a wide range of people involved in policy areas such as staff performance and health and safety;
Recruit staff;
Develop and implement policies on issues like working conditions, performance management, equal opportunities, disciplinary procedures and absence management;
Prepare staff handbooks;

Advise on pay and other remuneration issues, including promotion and benefits;

Conduct regular salary reviews;

Negotiate with staff and their representatives (for example, trade union officials) on issues relating to pay and conditions;

Manage payroll and maintaining employee records;

Interpret and advise on employment law;

Deal with complaints and implementing disciplinary procedures;

Develop with line managers HR planning strategies which consider immediate and long-term staff requirements;

Plan and deliver training

Analyze training needs in conjunction with departmental managers.

2- Recruitment Manager

The recruitment manager is responsible for the recruitment process. This process has to be properly designed and implemented. The manager sets recruitment measurement and distributes the job vacancies across HR recruiters. The manager builds a healthy relationship with internal customers and external recruitment vendors.

The recruitment manager is responsible for the development of the recruitment team in HR, develops successors, and increases the value added by the team members. The key responsibilities of a recruitment manager include the following:

Design and develop the recruitment process in the organization

Design the selection process for choosing the best recruitment method and recruitment source

Explore the market best practices in the recruitment and staffing and implement appropriate best practices in the company

Build a quality relationship with the internal customers and external recruitment agencies

Monitor and constantly reduces the costs of the recruitment process

Set the social media communication strategy for different job profiles and functions in the organization

Conduct job interviews for the managerial job positions monitors the labor legislation and implements required changes to keep the process compliant

Manage and develops the team of hr. recruiters

Act as a single point of contact for managers regarding recruitment topics

Design training recruitment for hr. recruiters and line managers

3- Development and Training Manager

The training manager is responsible for improving the productivity of an organization's employees. This position is responsible for the effective development, coordination, and presentation of training and development programs for all employees. The training manager assesses property-wide developmental needs to drive training initiatives, identifies, and arranges suitable training solutions for employees. This position actively searches, creatively designs and implements effective methods to educate, enhance performance and recognize performance. Typically, the essential functions of the manager include:

Conduct follow-up studies of all completed training to evaluate and measure results.

Modify programs as needed.

Develop effective training materials utilizing a variety of media.

Develop trainer development programs and coach others involved in training efforts, providing effective growth and development opportunities.

Develop and maintain property communications such as bulletin boards and newsletters to ensure employees have knowledge of property events and general information.

Plan, organize, facilitate and order supplies for employee events.

Develop and monitor spending against the departmental budget.

Exemplify the desired culture and philosophies of the organization.

Work effectively as a team member with other members of management and the human resources staff.

4- Employee relations manager

The employee relations manager is responsible for managing a range of activities related to employee labor relations and staffing functions. He or she manages the day-to-day activities and strategic support of employee relations programs for an organization. Typically, the functions of employee relations manager involve the following:

Manage classification plans and programs, arrange preparation of position descriptions, and conduct job evaluations.

Manage and interprets various labor agreements, administers grievance procedures; provides labor relations support during contract negotiations.

Act as a liaison between department managers and union representatives.

Provide advice and counsel to managers and supervisors regarding personnel practices, policy and employment laws.

Manage unemployment insurance processes; reviews liability reports and monitors program costs; and recommends policy changes to the director of human resources.

Manage the development of staffing strategies.

Develop and builds hiring processes for a variety of levels from temporary staffing to executive placement.

Develop, streamlines and enhances staffing systems, tracking reporting and analysis.

Lead sourcing and recruiting initiatives and processes to leverage networking and employee referrals.

Handle college relations and oversees various sourcing and internship programs.

Manage relocation, immigration and other responsibilities related to staffing administration.

Ensure compliance with all state and federal discrimination and employment regulations.

5- Health and Safety Manager

Health and safety officers use their knowledge and skills to promote a positive health and safety culture in the workplace. They are responsible for ensuring that employers and workers comply with safety legislation and that safety policies and practices are adopted and adhered to.

Health and safety officers are based in a wide range of organizations, from multinationals to small consultancies, and help to plan, implement, monitor, and review protective and preventative safety measures.

They work in partnership with employers, employees, directors, and trade unions to minimize: (1) operational losses; (2) occupational health problems; (3) accidents; (4) injuries.

Responsibilities vary depending on the employer and may cover, for example, fire safety or safe use of machinery or noise. However, duties typically involve:

Conduct risk assessments and considering how risks could be reduced;

Outlining safe operational procedures which identify and take account of all relevant hazards;

Conduct regular site inspections to check policies and procedures are being properly implemented;

Make changes to working practices that are safe and comply with legislation;

Preparing health and safety strategies and developing internal policy;

Lead internal training with managers and employees about health and safety issues and risks;

Keep records of inspection findings and producing reports that suggest improvements;

Record of incidents and accidents and producing statistics for managers;

Being up to date with new legislation and maintaining a working knowledge of all Health and Safety Executive (HSE) legislation and any developments that affect the employer's industry;

Attend Institution of Occupational Safety and Health (IOSH) seminars and reading professional journals;

Produce management reports, newsletters and bulletins;

Ensure the safe installation of equipment;

Manage and organizing the safe disposal of hazardous substances, e.g. asbestos;

Advise on a range of specialist areas, e.g. fire regulations, hazardous substances, noise, safeguarding machinery and occupational diseases.

6- Compensation and Benefits manager

HR compensation and benefits is responsible for overseeing the compensation and benefits division of a company. Analyzes compensation data within an organization and evaluates job positions to determine classification and salary. Administers employee insurance, pension and savings plans and works with insurance brokers and plan carriers. Typically, **the following function can be conducted by the compensation and benefits manager:**

Design, implement, and manage salary classification and compensation programs.

Conduct analysis of compensation and benefits within company.

Prepare occupational classifications, job descriptions, and salary scale.

Improve recruitment and retention.

Oversee competitive analysis, merit increases and salary structure.

Develop job descriptions for various positions and determine appropriate base pay.

Analyze surveys to ensure appropriate compensation across all departments.

Forecast budget for salary increases.

Manage employee insurance plans.

Manage pension and savings plans.

Advise on salary increase requests.

Negotiate collective agreements on behalf of employers or workers.

Research requirements and functional work, structural and functional relationships between jobs and occupations, and professional trends . Advise employees on state and federal employment regulations, collective agreements, benefits and compensation policies, personnel procedures and classification programs.

Based on above, the most important two careers are the HR officer, and compensation and benefits manager. This is because the HR officer has huge responsible in ensuring that the HR policies and strategies are conducted based on the interest of the organization. HR officer is responsible on recruiting the right person and placing him or her in the right position. Such act might enhance the organizational performance because right person in right position lead to right decision making and better utilizing of the resource and capabilities of the organization. The responsibilities of HR officers cover wide range of activities, which make his or her role very important to the organization. Choosing the wrong HR officers might lead to disastrous result that can affect the entire structure and operation of the organization. HR officers decided on the need of the organization of work force and recruit the right people to lead the organization to increase its productivity. Because of the above reason my first choice was the HR officers.

In recent years and particularly after the financial crises, many country and organization were asking to restructure the compensation and benefits that top management of organization gain. Some they related the crisis to the high benefits and compensation of top management. Employees started feeling that they are being treated unfairly. This has led to wide objections on the justice and fairness of employees and their management. Thus, my second choice is compensation and benefit manager. The responsibility of this manager is to make sure that employees are being compensated based on their performance and the compensation and benefits policies and strategies are fair and just for all the employees. This will lead to the feeling of being

25

treated fairly. Ultimately, this leads to more productive employees as well as organizations.

Human resources careers from another perceptive

1- Human resources officer:

The first official in charge of human resources for the development and implementation of official policies of human resources within the organization. Thus the HR officer has the right and the responsibility to observe and control the various human resources departments and units in order to ensure they follow the supreme policies and the action plans to achieve stated mutual goals.

2-Recruitment and selection manager:

The person who is committed to look for potential candidates with the desired knowledge, skills and experience to allow an organization to select the most appropriate and people to fill job vacancies.

His/her usual tasks include:

-Determining the job vacancies and their requirements.

-Designing a plan for attracting potential people to apply for those jobs. The plan could include advertising on TV or radio channels, newspapers, magazines, electronic web sites and some labor agencies and unions may help in this process.

-Using scientific tools in order to choose the best and suitable employees among all those applicants who are hoping to be chosen. These scientific tools may include:

Job interviews –job exams-the previous practical experiences –educational level-the languages spoken –the psychological readiness for the job.

The main purpose of the recruitment process is to find the widest pool of applicants to provide the greatest opportunity to select the best people for the required roles in an organization.

3- Development and training manager

 Analyzing, planning, and developing internal and external training courses for their employees. Trainers help educate employees in necessary job skills and for advancement. They also create training manuals, procedures, and training aids for the organization. Training programs can range from sales techniques, marketing, communication skills, meetings and time management, particular needed languages, new updates related to the field of the organization's work or activities to safety issues. So they design the training plan in terms of its duration, curriculum, expected benefits and the history and reputation of the trainers or the training agency which would be chosen.

4-Employee relations manager:

ER manager is the person who works as a bridge between the organization and the employees. Moreover, employee relations cover all communications between the business·owner and the employees from the HR perspective. Also, as it is known, ER managers are always trying to fill the gap between the employees and the top management as well as making employees' voice demands heard.

Also employee relations managers supposed to represent the employees in the labor unions, seminars and conferences. Moreover, ER managers have social roles and responsibilities toward the employees in case of being in trouble such as: family problems, illness and financial problems. Furthermore, ER managers engaged in solving some problems and conflicts among employees, which occur in the workplace because of different factors such as: misunderstanding, lack of fruitful communications and unclear rules etc.....

In addition to the above mentioned, the biggest challenge could face ER manager is that how to build an effective citizenship culture which is considered to be a great factor makes organizations more effective, competitive and successful. The best example which interpret the importance of having an effective citizenship culture within the organization is applied over there at the Japanese companies as they are known for having loyal employees who are very loyal to the organizations that they working for, that big loyalty makes a lot of Japanese employees putting their companies' flags and the national flag of Japan together on their homes, cars and as a mobile or PC background.

5-health and safety manager:

The Health and Safety Section of the Human Resources Department is responsible for:

Ensuring that the organization meets its obligations with all occupational safety and health statutes and regulations.

- Facilitating employee participation in Health & Safety.

- Monitoring the Health & Safety performance across the University and reporting on this to senior management along with relevant recommendations for improvement.

-Health and safety education aimed at empowering departments to effectively   identify and manage the hazards in their area.

- Develop health and safety programs

6-compensation and benefits specialist:

-Responsible for designing, managing and controlling the compensation and benefits policies and regulations within the organization which include rewards, bonuses, incentives, as well as salaries.-

 -Oversee pension and savings plans, Advice on salary increase requests and Forecast budget for salary increases.

-Administering and managing employee's insurance.

-Analyzing surveys to ensure appropriate compensation across all departments.

In my opinion, the two best Human resources careers are the following ones:

1-Training and development manager **(my preferred choice):**

Personally, if I were asked to choose among human resources careers, I would select to be a training and development manager for the following reasons:

-HR training and development managers are known globally for getting high salaries, bonuses and reward as well.

-They always have the opportunities to visit different foreign countries particularly to manage the external training courses for their organization's employees.

-Having opportunities in working abroad and international experience.

-HR management is considered as a wide managerial specialization which includes a lot of sub-specialization below it .So, people who are intending to do PHD degree in Human resources, mostly find it very interesting and promising to do their PHD topic on HR training and how to developed the intellectual capital which employees carry around in their heads,strengthing their skills and abilities and finding new methods to replace the routine and the usual work practices with the creative thinking which makes the organization having the capability of being competitive and innovative.

-Personally, I have been planning for my near future which begins (Inca Allah) after my graduation from IUKL with MBA-human resources management .So, I decided to take some specialized courses in HR training and development management to support my CV and my opportunity to get a high position job in a national or international company as well as to get sufficient knowledge which strongly equipping me to do my PHD degree.

2-Employee relations manager **(my second choice)**

One of my desired job choices is to be an employee relations manager, because it is very beneficial for me specially in building my political future as the one of the ER manager's tasks to be like a bridge between the employees and the labor unions and the government.

For instance, in some circumstances such as job strikes, the employee relations managers are supposed to do their best to resolve the problems that employees suffer from and to engage in negotiations as a representative of the employees who are demanding their rights such as: Increasing their wages, getting medical or life insurance, decreasing working hours.

Furthermore, this career administers and interprets various labor agreements, administers grievance procedures, provide labor relations support during contract negotiations.

Also it is filling the gap between department managers and union representatives. Thus working in this branch of human resources management will probably be my first steps to the world of politics with a strong experience in how such those economic and labor issues are solved by the legislation and the government intervention.

In addition to my main criteria to choose this career, which is getting ready to enter the door of politics, also this career is considered as a one of the most paying jobs.

Do you think employees can be objective enough in measuring their own worth to reach accurate conclusions about fairness of their pay?

I strongly believe that, most of employees over the world are not objective in evaluating their pay and benefits. Employees are mostly used to overestimate their knowledge, skills, abilities, experience and their role importance. In contrast, employees tend to underestimate their salaries, bonuses and other benefits provided by their employer. Often employees expect their pay to cover basic living expenses, keep up with inflation, leave some money for savings or recreation and expect it to increase over time. On the other hand, employees usually do not consider that their employers are frequently affected by a lot of problems in their market which may probably lead the organization to make a loss, financial crisis which might prevent the employer to higher the pay and the other benefits for the employees. Employee's dissatisfaction may arise if either internal or external equity principles are violated. Simply put, internal equity refers to the relative fairness of wages received by other employees in the same organization. External equity is fairness relative to wages outside the organization.

The issue of fairness is critical to compensation administration and most every phase of labor management. Generally, workers and managers agree, in principle, that wages should take into account a job's required preparation, responsibility, and even unpleasantness and performance differences or seniority. Less agreement exists about the relative importance of each of these factors. Challenges in applying differential payment system from subjectivity in the evaluations of both jobs and employees. In evaluating the fairness of their pay, employees balance *inputs such as* work effort, skills against *outcomes* such as pay, compensation, privileges. Employees may seek balance in the following six ways:

1-modify input or output if underpaid, a person may reduce his effort *or* try to obtain a raise if overpaid, a person may increase efforts or employee longer hours without additional compensation.

2-adjust the notion of what is fair if overpaid, an employee may think himself the recipient of other benefits such as doing interesting work if overpaid, an employee may come to believe he deserves it

3- Change source of equity comparison, an employee who has compared himself with a promoted co-worker may begin to compare himself with another worker.

4- Attempt to change the input or output of others asking others not to work so hard.

5- Withdraw (through increased absenteeism, mental withdrawal or quitting.

6- Forcing others to withdraw (trying to obtain a transfer for a co-worker or force him to quit).

In my conclusion, employees as human beings always want everything as a price for doing something regardless its value. In this case , some religions specially the Islam prohibits its followers to request having wages which is more than what they actually deserve(greed).In other words, some employees would remain dissatisfied with their job pay and benefits as long as they comparing themselves with their counterparts within the same organization or in other organizations without taking into their account the differences among them in terms of educational levels, skills, abilities, experience and other job requirements.

On the other hand, some employers are trying to employ workforce with low wages in order to decrease the cost of their products or services to achieve as much as profits possible. As a result, this unethical and unlawful act might negatively affect the behavior of employees which may lead some of them to behave unethically without feeling guilt .Moreover, some employers and their employees seem to be playing the supplier – customer game, where the supplier desires to sell with the highest possible price and the customers doing their best in order to buy with the lowest possible price.

How can an employer address biases in employees perceptions about pay?

Because of the negative effects on the productivity and organizational effectiveness caused by employees' dissatisfaction on their pay and benefits, so all employers are committed to clear and justify the underlying reasons of that problem in order to solve this misunderstanding which is necessarily should be resolved as soon as possible and should not avoid it to keep the employees on the right track and help keeping them away from following unethical behavior.

Also, employers should have enough knowledge about the influences of pay problems which might influence the motivation, loyalty and desire of their employees and its influence on the employer business's profits. In the rest of developing and developed countries ,there are well designed labor laws which control the and organize the relationship between the workers and their employers in terms of the minimum wages rate , insurance, safety and health, layoff ,bonuses and other related aspects. So these laws could help solving problems related to wages as these legislations are equally dealing the two sides based on the rights- responsibilities equation. Moreover, in some circumstances like financial crisis some companies are not able to pay for their employees which bring them under the fire, then they should communicate with their employees and explain the case which company is suffering from in order to keep the employees in the company and reaching a mutual agreement which might probably include cutting or postponing the wages, pausing the bonuses and other unnecessary expenses until ending up the crisis.

Furthermore, some greedy employees should be asked to appreciate their companies as a part of loyalty to their organization and also should be required to be more productive in order to make the organization making extra profits which might help increase the wages of employees. As well as ,they are should be advised to avoid comparing themselves with others inside or outside the organization without taking into their accounts that their counterparts might be more skilled , highly educated, hardworking and other considerations related to seniority.

(Department of Accounting, College of Administration and Economics/ University of Basra, Iraq)
hisham noori hussain AL-hashimy   978-1-62265-912-8 (online) 978-1-62265-913-5 (paper)

If you worked for a business that wanted to promote a valued employee but had no more money in the payroll budget, how would you address the issue of fairness <u>in this situation? How would you expect the employee to respond?</u>

Our business: Abdul-Charles-Karol private schools chain

Our problem: having not enough money to promote a valued employee

Introduction

In harsh economic times, most companies start to examine how they can cut costs and save cash, with eyes almost inevitably turning to the company's employee wage bill which will invariably take a large chunk out of the company coffers each week or month. The thought of just cutting wage levels across the board by a certain percentage to save money must sometimes be very tempting for bosses or by cutting the pay of underperforming employees. Sadly for employers, employment law dictates that workers' pay can only be cut with their express agreement. This is because an employee's level of pay must form part of their employment contract (which could be written, oral or implied by the actions of you and the employee) so reducing their pay would amount to a variation of contract which you cannot do unless the employee agrees.

Our solution

In my case, if my company is in serious financial trouble, I will decide to ask, only our senior staff above a certain level to take a pay cut, or I might need to ask for a cut across the board. If possible I will ask our employees to appoint a representative who will be responsible for coming to an agreement with us which will then be binding on all staff.

To get our valued employee and his /her coworkers to agree it might be an idea to offer them some incentives which could include:

A promise to return pay and other promotions (rewards-holiday tickets-clothes-mobile phone bills) to original levels once things start improving.

34

Reduced hours.

Flexible working arrangements.

Allowing employees to buy extra holiday days.

Appreciation certificate.

Our employee's response

In this case, I will think of various scenarios because expecting how the valued employee will respond basically depends on the employee himself in terms of his/her loyalty, personality, available job chances. In other words, the employee has the option to be loyal and sacrifice in order to save his organization and struggle with other coworkers to rescue their organization or to leave it once it begins suffering to another organization which offers better benefits. Actually, if my business is expected to face such this problem, I would prefer it to be running in Japan. Because as mentioned in relevant studies conducted on this area the highest employees satisfaction and loyalty levels are found in the Japanese companies where employees are mostly ready to sacrifice for their organizations. Also they put the flags of their organization on roofs of their houses as a sign of love and loyalty toward their employer.

providing reasonable accommodation to disabled employees in an organization.

A reasonable accommodation is assistance or changes to a position or workplace that will enable an employee to do his or her job despite having a disability. The employers are required to provide reasonable accommodations to qualified employees with disabilities, unless doing so would pose an undue hardship. Qualified employees are those who hold the necessary degrees, skills, and experience for the job; and who can perform its essential functions, with or without an accommodation. Reasonable accommodations can apply to the duties of the job or where and how job tasks are performed. The accommodation should make it easier for the employee to successfully perform the duties of the position. In case of disable employee, the accommodation must be customized to suit them so that they can perform their job more effectively.

Examples of accommodations include:

The first example including the adjustment of existing facilities in the workplace so that the disable employees can use these facilities. This can include the installment of computer screen magnifiers so that an employee with weak sight can see the writing on the computers or those who cannot hear (deaf), the employer can install for them telecommunication tools that can help them in understanding others who trying to communicate with them. One important adjustment is installing a reader for those who cannot read because they are blind.

Another example of reasonable accommodations is the restructuring of jobs. This could be including allowing different working hours so that those with disabilities can work longer to afford time for their medical treatment. For example, employers can adjust the working time from 8 hours a day to 10 hours a day so that the employee will work for 4 days a week and will have three days to attend to issue for his or her medical treatment.

Describe what will happen if the above (1) is not provided

The goals of providing reasonable accommodation are to provide the employees with facilities so that they can do their work better. If the employers did not provide the employees with reasonable accommodation, there are many consequences. These include the productivity of the employees, as they will not feel motivated to do the work. A blind employee without reader will not be able to do anything so that the prohibition of providing reasonable accommodation will lead to the exclusion of the employees from the workforce.

Another issue that the employer might face is from legal perspectives. Most of the laws around the world encourage the employers to provide the reasonable accommodation for those who are in need. Not doing so will expose the employer to be sued in the court and provide compensation for the damages that he or she caused for the disabled employees. In addition, those who need special treatment they might be expose to have unfavorable incident such as death case due to not being able to have proper and timely medical treatment, this might expose the employer to be the responsible of the death and lead him or her to jail.

From marketing perspective, the employers will have bad reputation if he or she does not provide reasonable accommodation. Employee will spread the word and the employer has to face the outrage of public regarding not being socially responsible. This might affect the public picture of the employer and lead some customer to boycott the product or services of the employers.

Training

Training is a solution. A training programme can be created by using the ADDIE model.

Firstly, an assessment has to be done on what are the job related needs required by the employees to encourage team building. The assessment also must evaluate what existing knowledge participants have, and also defines the gap between what they know and what they need to know.

Secondly, Harry need to come up with a training design that meets the employees' and employer's needs. Content design, resource evaluation and a training plan needs to be drawn up. In this case, where team building and team work needs to be emphasized on, the content and learning outcomes should bring the team together.

Training development with the appropriate activities to encourage team building should be inserted into the programme. The activities could include games sessions such as a game of futsal, or solving problems in given

(Department of Accounting, College of Administration and Economics/ University of Basra, Iraq)
hisham noori hussain AL-hashimy   978-1-62265-912-8 (online) 978-1-62265-913-5 (paper)

scenarios to encourage employees to discuss amongst each other as well as provide support to their team mates. Informative motivational seminars and forums can also help build an excellent work team, and as such, should be inserted into the training programme.

Thirdly, in implementing the training programme, proper trainers should be selected to deliver the training. Trainers should be able to break the ice in any group as well as focus on the required outcome of the training programme. The trainer should also be fluent in addressing team building hiccups such as miscommunication, cold feet and lack of participation from the employees.

At the end, an evaluation needs to be conducted to see if the team responded positively to the training session, and that the training session could increase the productivity of the company through the much needed team work.

Total Quality Management (TQM)

Managers are often reluctant to implement TQM programs as they believe the money involved will be excessive, and that management's time on implementation may be harmful to production. On the other hand, managers recognize that TQM is not always synonymous with quality. Whereas quality is about unbending focus, passion, iron discipline and a way of life for all, TQM is often more about jargon, documentation, committees and quality departments. Some of the major reasons that TQM programs do not work, even in organizational environments is because of its focus on internal processes rather than external results, focus on minimum standards and its huge administration.

The first of the four conditions that an organization could find useful in self-managed teams

Is that the quality of work improves, the speed of work processes increase, resulting in more innovative and creative output by the organisation. The better the team works together, the better the image of the organisation. Secondly, greater team motivation reduces operational costs within the organisation through reduction in managerial or supervisory roles. The third condition an organisation could find useful would be increased efficiencies and greater employee job satisfaction resulting in increased commitment and productivity. Organisation would not need to go out in search of new team member replacements every few years, spend on advertising for vacant roles and such. Lastly, the organisation would experience lower turnover and absenteeism rate, which is very important and useful, as employees within the team find their roles worthwhile and job secure.

Managers can develop high-performance work teams

 By evaluating what is needed to make the required improvements. For example, if team work is found lacking, managers could provide adequate training so team member skills and experiences match team building requirements. They could also provide objective goals, incentives using the appropriate resources. Other than that, they can ensure that the organization has the necessary resources to commit to this kind of change in time, money, and people. Managers should pay close attention to team design decisions. They can develop team-based measurements and corresponding feedback methods that address team performance methods that address team performance. Lastly, they could recruit and train managers to act as facilitators or coaches.

From organization point of view, there are several important fairness issues that involved in deciding how to handle the lateness issue.

When a fair system is implemented as part of organization core value, it able to create a culture of fair treatment among employees and lead to company performance. In overall perspective, there are three fairness issues and dimensions that RPJ Restaurant needs to consider in solving the lateness issues. Firstly, it is about procedural fairness. Procedural fairness refers to fairness of decision by having formal procedure and policies. An action in handling lateness will consider fair if the action are taken as balanced and correct. Balance are referring to similar actions are taken in similar situations

(Department of Accounting, College of Administration and Economics/ University of Basra, Iraq)
hisham noori hussain AL-hashimy   978-1-62265-912-8 (online)   978-1-62265-913-5 (paper)

and correctness with quality, clarity, consistency. This is important as such procedure is a written policies that tells staff about the consequences of lateness and it ensures all staff been acknowledged. Those factors, information and monitoring methods are being communicated to staff. Staff is more likely to accept responsibilities, consequences at the same time satisfied if procedures are fair.

Secondly, RPJ restaurant also need to understand interactional fairness issue. Interactional is defined as the thoroughness of information provided as well as amount of dignity and respected demonstrated during taking action on the staff involved in lateness. It involves the personal touch in the interaction process with staff together with facts and records. If management wants to penalize a staff for being late, a record of lateness frequency, warning letter issued with correct manners. When consequence actions are taken with negative interaction ally unfair, the staff involves are likely to develop negative attitudes towards the management, system and policies in the RPJ Restaurant. The affected staff should be given an opportunity to input and response with their stories to the misconduct. This illustrated both way interaction in such decision making process.

Lastly, RPJ also needs to take into account the fairness in term of compliance to regulations and labor laws. There is a regulation and law to protect the work force and it is very important for a company to comply with such regulations as part of compliance. In process of monitoring the employees' compliance, record of consequence management, need to be accordance to the regulation guideline. This is to ensure the staff involved felt what company done is fairly accordance to regulations. Company must able to provide effected employees with rational of decision, unbiased processing of facts and regulation criteria in decision making. Besides, this is also able to demonstrate the fairness of company on every staff that committed the same mistake.

In the perspective of company, they are able to make it a fair policies and implementation.

 However, in the view of employees' and other servers, the idea of fairness could be different. Firstly, in the eyes of employees, fairness means treating everyone the same. Employees will see a decision is fair if they see the same decision is made for other employees with the same misconduct. For example, in term of lateness, if a staff been given a warning letter after 10 times late in a month, they expect to see the same action on the another staff with the same lateness offence. So from here, they will see company is treating everyone the same without consideration of sex, position or race. It applies the same with another situation where 5 same levels of servers in RPJ restaurant should have the same salary package, number of annual leaves, allowance payment. Server A in restaurant who has the same level with Server B should have same remuneration packages. However, company need to acknowledge that several factors such as number of service years, experience and others might affect such packages.

Secondly, in some view of employees, fairness means giving the people what they deserve. Some employees might argue that people that perform better and contribute more to the company should be treated better as compared to low performers. This is because the staff has contribute more their time and afford to the company. For example, if all staff gets the same increment in terms of salary regardless of performance differences, top performers will see it as unfair as others are not providing results as they are. Top performers think they deserve more increment, recognition and treatment as they have done more to the company. Who provide more effort and result should be compensated with more compensation. In this perspective, RPJ restaurants should have standardized criteria in the merit-based pay scheme so that all staff able to have same opportunity and understand the decision making behind.

Lastly, some employees view fairness means giving the people what they need. This perspective is not clear cut as previous two ideas of fairness as no rigid formula behind this idea. Such fairness idea might relate to social

41

status, medical condition, even physical difference of different staff. In some circumstances, employees are able to except the idea where better treatment been given to staff who need them. For example, staff that pregnant should be given a special parking place as compared to others as they not convenient to walk much. Servers that have physical imparity and limitation should be given chances if they late to work while others should be punctual to work. Under such circumstance, each staff that different much be treated differently so that it is fair as a whole.

Question 2 (16 marks)

A member of the RPJ restaurant's serving staff is chronically late for work.

a) From the organization's point of view (RPJ), what fairness issues are involved in deciding how to handle this situation?

(8 marks)

b) In what ways might the employees' and other servers' ideas of fairness be different? You may use appropriate examples to support your answers.

(8 marks)

Question 3 a)

The flexible budget for production and sale of 900 units are as below:

Fixed cost for 900 units = RM 180,000

Variable cost for 900 units = RM 414,000

Flexible budget   = Fixed cost + Variable cost * unit

= 180,000 + 414,000

= RM 594,000

Question 3 (25 Marks)

GAMUDA MACHINERY
Budgeted Operating Income for October 2012

	Master (Static) Budget
Units	1000
	RM
Sales	800,000
Variable costs	450,000
Contribution margin	350,000
Fixed costs	150,000
Operating income	200,000

Gamuda Machinery manufactured and sold 900 units for RM 840 each in December. The company incurred RM 414,000 total variable expenses and RM 180,000 total fixed expenses.

Required:

(a)   Prepare a flexible budget for the production and sale of 900 units.

(6 marks)

(b)   Compute the sales volume variance, in term of operating income and contribution margin.

(6 marks)

(c)   Compute for December:
    (i)   The total flexible budget variance
    (ii)   The total variable cost flexible budget variance
    (iii)   The total fixed cost flexible budget variance
    (iv)   The selling price variance

(8 marks)

(d)   Explain how standard cost and flexible budgets can be used for short-term profit analysis such as for financial control purposes.

(5 marks)

-END OF QUESTION PAPER-

43

Choose two cultural activities of the main ethnic groups (Malay-Indian Chinese) in Malaysia and justify?

Personally, the most activities which I admired here in Malaysia are the various methods which the three ethnic groups (Malay-Chinese-Indians) use in preparing their unique dishes (food) and the second activity is that how they celebrate their weddings .my justifications for choosing to write on food preparation and wedding celebrations in Malaysia are related to my personal interests which definitely include food preparation process among different cultures and nations. So it seems interesting to know detailed information about ingredients used by Malaysians while preparing their food and how it tastes. Also how the others who are their cultural, ethnic and religious backgrounds are different from mine celebrate their grooms and brides during engagement and marriage days.

Describe in detail similarities and differences in (i) that exists in your ethnic group?

Activity 1: Food preparation

First group: Chinese

Introduction

Malaysian Chinese eat all types of food, including Chinese, Indian, Malay and Western cuisines. Few Malaysian Chinese are vegetarians, and those who do are usually devout adherents of Buddhism. Malaysian Chinese food contains similarities and differences with the Chinese food in China. Malaysian Chinese food is similar to the food in Southern China as it is primarily derived from the Hokier, Cantonese, Hakka and Teaches cuisines.

Figure 1: Back Cut the from Clang (Malaysian Chinese food

A number of traditional Chinese dishes have been developed, either by the use of local ingredients or through fresh invention, into local specialty. For example, there are local inventions such as Lon Me, thick noodles in clear gravy (in the Clang Valley) and dark gravy (in Penang). Back Cut the originated from Clang and not China. Street food such as char way tow and Hainan's chicken rice commonly found in Malaysia and Singapore are distinctive to the region. During Chinese New Year, Malaysian Chinese will also eat Hushing which was developed mainly in Kuala Lumpur.

Malaysian Chinese food preparations compared to those in my ethnic group (Arab):

To be honest, it is might be impossible to find similarities between the different kinds of food prepared by Malaysian Chinese and those dishes prepared by Arabs. As I believe , the underlying reasons of that refers to the cultural gap between Chinese around the world and Arab because of the far distance between the two geographical regions (China and the middle east). So as I think, the ingredients and taste of both of them are totally different. In Middle East, People tend to add a lot of spices and some parts of plants and flowers to their food. Also, Arab tends to mix their food with meat and chicken (particularly beef, lamb and camel's meat) than being vegetarian as a lot of Chines are. The only similarity could exists maybe is that the two ethnic groups are always use the rice in their main traditional and modern dishes.

(Department of Accounting, College of Administration and Economics/ University of Basra, Iraq)
hisham noori hussain AL-hashimy   978-1-62265-912-8 (online) 978-1-62265-913-5 (paper)

Figure 2: Arab Caps consists of rice, meat, Rabbi and nuts.

Second group: Malaysian Indians

There are plenty of similarities between the Indian food and the Arab food. The main reason of that is the close distance between India and the countries of Arab Gulf (Saudi Arabia, Kuwait, Emirates, Oman and Qatar). From centuries ago, it is well know that the trade between the two sides is very active. The traders from the two groups (Arab and Indians) were actively trading off the items and products manufactured in their countries such as: rice, spices, carpets, clothes and traditional weapons. Hence, the two groups have explored how each one of them prepares food in terms of what ingredients to use and at what level of amount to add ingredients as well as at what season to make it because some dishes which require special ingredients are related to specific seasons.

(Department of Accounting, College of Administration and Economics/ University of Basra, Iraq)
hisham noori hussain AL-hashimy   978-1-62265-912-8 (online) 978-1-62265-913-5 (paper)

Third group: Malay

If Malay food is to be described in just a few words, the most appropriate may be – "A festival of flavors". Having absorbed various cultural influences through the centuries, particularly Chinese, Indian, Arab, Thai and Indonesian, Malay cuisine has evolved into its very own. What gives Malay food its main and unmistakable characteristic is the expert use of remap, which is a mixture of wet and dry herbs and spices. Indeed, many popular Malay dishes begin with a ground paste consisting of red onion or shallots, garlic, ginger, galangal, fresh turmeric and lemongrass. In addition to this, is the famed dry spice combo of star anise, cinnamon sticks, cardamom and cloves? Because of the religious links between the native people of Malaysia (Malay) and Arab and its accumulative reflection on their cultures, a lot of Malaysian and Arabian dishes are considered to be attractive and acceptable to the members of two ethnic groups.

Figure 3: Malaysian street sellers selling local dishes.

Activity 2: wedding celebrations

First group: Malay

(Department of Accounting, College of Administration and Economics/ University of Basra, Iraq)
hisham noori hussain AL-hashimy   978-1-62265-912-8 (online) 978-1-62265-913-5 (paper)

The activities that take place during a Malay wedding come from the diverse cultural traditions --indigenous, Hindu and Islamic--that have together served to shape traditional Malay culture. The numerous activities constitute a Malay wedding may be conveniently be divided into three groups representing three stages. The first group of activities, all of which precede the actual wedding ceremony, consist of   (a) the investigation   (meristic), (b) the engagement or approach to formalize the arrangement (demining), and (c) the hanta ran or the sending of gifts and part of the amount of money (Wang Belinda) for expenses (Wang Belinda) which the boy's family give to the girl's side that will be incurred by the girl's family.

Figure 4: the platform of the groom and his wife where they sit during wedding ceremony.
This photo is taken to a pattern shown in the national Malaysian museum.

The Wang Belinda is usually an amount of several thousand ringgits. It is different from the dowry (mas chawing) which is also paid by the man to his future wife. The amount of the mas chawing is usually fixed by the Islamic Religious Council in each state, but a potential bridegroom may give any amount above the official figure.

48

The second group of activities consists of the actual marriage ceremony (acid nice) and biryani, while the third group of activities consists of barrack or arriving in procession, sitting on a decorated dais (bersanding and the welcoming of the married couple to the bride's house (Sabot meant).

In Libya, the traditions of weddings seem to be very close to their counterparts in the Malaysian culture. The similarities such as:

1- All stages like investigation, engagement and sending the gifts are existing in the Libyan traditions.

2- The family of groom should provide the bride of son some amount of money in order to buy some clothes and gold and other things needed as new wife.

3- The same Islamic rules are followed in my country such as: signing the certificate of marriage by at least one representative from bride's family and another one from the groom's family.

On the other hand, the Libyan traditions are relatively different in terms of days of celebration, local music, and local dances. Also, we have a tradition called (Seurat Alafia reading day).

Figure 5: Libyan traditional band performing local dances with music belongs to (Zukav music)

The second and third groups (Chinese and Indians):

Because of the influence which religious beliefs and cultures have on wedding ceremonies over the nations, the weddings of Malaysian Indians and Chinese are totally different from Arabian weddings. The rest of non-Muslims Malaysians (Chinese and Indians) are following Hinduism and Buddhism which finally lead us to know that their traditions during wedding day and marriage celebrations are not similar to ours as affected by the rules of the religions which they follow. Moreover, the weddings will be affected by the traditions and ancient folklore which they carried during their migrations from their original countries to Malaysia.

Explain ways managers can deal with such diversities (culture, gender, religion) in the workplace.

Introduction

Diversity as a Vital Resource, diversity is defined as "otherness or those human qualities that are different from our own and outside the groups to which we belong, yet present in other individuals and groups." Dimensions of diversity include, but are not limited to: age, ethnicity, ancestry, gender, physical abilities/qualities, race, sexual orientation, educational background, geographic location, income, marital status, military experience, religious beliefs, parental status, and work experience (Olden and Rosenberg 1991, 18-19). It's important to understand how these dimensions affect performance, motivation, success, and interactions with others. Institutional structures and practices that have presented barriers to some dimensions of diversity should be examined, challenged, and removed.

Figure 6: shows diversity in a workplace where the workforce is different in terms of: age, gender, race, physical status and other standards.

Diversity in the workplace is important to running a successful business .Heterogeneous groups deliver better solutions and critical analysis, so you must structure and run your company in a way that promotes diversity. By adopting the attitude of "not seeing color," you run the risk of treating people insensitively. You must recognize that people have differences, be they physical, generational or cultural, and you cannot pretend that these barriers have been broken down. Instead, celebrate the differences among your employees, and encourage them to let their individualities show. For example, don't hesitate to ask someone from another culture about their culture's etiquette practices, so, their knowledge could prove useful to your business.

(Department of Accounting, College of Administration and Economics/ University of Basra, Iraq)
hisham noori hussain AL-hashimy   978-1-62265-912-8 (online) 978-1-62265-913-5 (paper)

Considerations and Warnings for businesses with diverse workforce:

As workplaces become more diverse, employers are encouraged to take note of communication, training, recruiting practices and management. Diverse workforces may be plagued with problems if employees aren't equipped with the knowledge they need to communicate effectively with their coworkers, regardless of their differences. Diversity training can help reduce interpersonal conflicts within a company. As a result of

Efforts to train employees on diversity issues, management may see an increase in training and development costs.

1- Recognition

You must recognize that people have differences, such as their physical, generational or cultural backgrounds, and you cannot pretend that these barriers have been broken down. Instead, celebrate the differences among your employees, and encourage them to let their individualities show.

2- Fairness:

Acting fairly and acting uniformly are different, and only one enables you to successfully deal with diversity in your workplace. Don't be fooled into thinking that by treating everyone exactly the same, you are demonstrating a fair attitude and respecting diversity. Instead, treat people fairly and respect the differences that make them who they are. For example, don't schedule a mandatory meeting that falls on a religious holiday.

3- Encouraging the Interaction:

When you identify diversity-related issues in the workplace, discuss them with your employees in a no confrontational manner. For example, encourage employees to work with others of different backgrounds or generations. Initiating these types of interactions encourages your employees to learn more about communication styles, talents and goals - their own and those of their co-workers.

4- Employee Assessments

As a manager or business owner, you probably already conduct employee reviews and assessments. When preparing these reviews, you must also examine your employees' attitudes, particularly how they work with others. If you notice that an employee only delegates tasks to people of a certain race, or if an employee discounts the ideas of people below or above a certain age, it is your responsibility to address the issue. Identify issues among your employees and bring them up when assessing their performance.

5- Diversity related conflicts prevention:

With being so beneficial to business, diversity might have adverse effects when it is not managed well by the managers who are not having enough knowledge about managing diverse workforce. So some conflicts might probably occur among employees because of their differences.

Explain advantages and disadvantages of knowing ones cultural differences in terms of promoting goods and services.

Give specific examples to support your explanation.

Introduction

The cultural, religious and ethnic differences could affect the promotion of products and goods in two different ways (positively and negatively). Since the cultural and religious principles and traditions are still playing a significant role in forming the behavior and perspectives of people as the majority of societies across the world tend to be traditional societies where the traditions and the religious rules are still a hot line (taboo). In contrast, there are some societies are increasingly breaking their obligations toward the rules of their cultures and religions. For instance, European people and those living in USA and Canada where the western culture is dominant.

Cultural differences advantages in terms of promoting products and services:

1- As mentioned above, the Cultural differences have many different meanings. Culture can cut across nationality and religions. It gives group of people their own identity, art, thought, language and social activity. As a

(Department of Accounting, College of Administration and Economics/ University of Basra, Iraq)
hisham noori hussain AL-hashimy   978-1-62265-912-8 (online) 978-1-62265-913-5 (paper)

result, people are believed to be proud of their own traditions and heritage which create a lot of opportunities to business owners around the world to promote their products and services .For instance, Schools in USA and UK always are aware of the importance and benefits of valuing and promoting cultural diversity with children. It is important that we understand cultural diversity of children within the school. Then we will be able to help children of their learning to their own lives.

 In other words, in the British schools and educational services centers provide opportunities for the spiritual, moral, social and cultural education of its children to ensure that they understand and value social and cultural diversity in Britain and the world. An essential part of preparation for adult life is preparation to live in a multi-ethnic, multicultural and multi-faith society.

2- Some religious rules make a chance to some businesses to promote some relevant products which attractive to people who follow those rules. For example, in non- Muslim countries where there are Muslim communities and students such as: USA, UK, Australia and other western countries, some food businesses and restaurant chains hunted the chance and provided a lot of kind of canned food, meat and dishes which meet the Islamic conditions in terms of being pork free and the way how the animals are killed. So, they offer Halal products like Macdonald and KFC fast food restaurants which have opening new branches of Halal food in areas where Muslim communities are intensively existed in some countries.

3- Also companies around the world usually organize advertising campaigns as a promotion tool to attract people buy their products during seasonal festivals and cultural celebrations such as: Chinese New Year, Enid Alfieri, Christmas and Halloween.

Cultural differences disadvantages in terms of promoting products and services:

In the business world, communication is imperative for the successful execution of daily operations. Understanding cultural differences and overcoming language barriers are some of the considerations people should

(Department of Accounting, College of Administration and Economics/ University of Basra, Iraq)
hisham noori hussain AL-hashimy   978-1-62265-912-8 (online) 978-1-62265-913-5 (paper)

have when dealing with business with people of various cultures. Often business deals are lost because the parties involved did not take the time to learn about their each other's cultures prior to interacting. When launching a promotion campaign or advertising to members of a different culture, always research the target market prior to beginning the campaign. Levels of conservatism, gender views and ideologies can vary greatly between cultures. Presenting a campaign that is not in line with specific cultural norms can insult the target audience and greatly hinder the campaign. Being aware of cultural norms can also help your company narrow down the target audience. For instance, in Japan and Austria, men usually are in control of decision making, but women make the majority of purchasing decisions in Sweden.

Cultural barriers. Subtle cultural differences may make an ad that tested well in one country unsuitable in another—e.g., an ad that featured a man walking in to join his wife in the bathroom was considered an inappropriate invasion in Japan. Symbolism often differs between cultures, and humor, which is based on the contrast to people's experiences, tends not to travel well. Values also tend to differ between cultures—in the U.S. and Australia, excelling above the group is often desirable, while in Japan, "The nail that sticks out gets hammered down." In the U.S., "The early bird gets the worm" while in China "The first bird in the flock gets shot down."

In my conclusion, promotion of goods and services is definitely affected by the differences among people in terms of their cultural backgrounds .For instance , one American fast food chain wanted to add some new promoted dishes which include some non- Halal ingredients to its lists at its branches in Muslim countries such as : Lebanon , Algeria , Tunisia and Libya, but the company could not get a permission from the authorities in both governments of Algeria and Libya because of the culture and religious beliefs in these countries are dominant as the people there are considered to be conservative. On the other hand it could get the permission to offer the new dishes in Lebanon and Tunisia as the culture there is different from that in Libya and Algeria because Tunisia and Lebanon are applying secular

55

system and a large proportion of people there either secularists, western culture oriented or non- Muslims .

Inter-active computer training and experiential training program

Introduction

The importance of training is now recognized in all progressive organizations. Some companies have fixed a certain minimum amount of training as mandatory for career advancement of their officers and executives. Management training develops employee strengths and their ability to contribute within the organization. A variety of management training is available in organizations – choices are endless. The management training can include internally supplied, customized for your company, on-going management development. The importance of employee training doesn't end with new workers. Manager training and development is equally important to workplace safety, productivity, and satisfaction. Among the most useful skills that can be addressed are manager communication, employee motivation, and employee recognition, teamwork skills as well as leadership skills.

But managers are busy people, and that's why manager training online using Training is such an effective means of keeping your supervisors at their best. Online training is also an efficient way to help break experienced workers of sloppy - and possibly unsafe - work habits.

Trainers should research their company's situation thoroughly before developing a customized training plan for a company. You can use many different company resources to help you determine your company's training needs, such as company goals, HR complaints and legal obligations.

A successful training program is always a work in progress, and the training cycle isn't complete without an evaluation of training's effectiveness, which leads to decision-making and planning for future training. Here are several methodologies for evaluation as well as practical ways to retrieve good results.

Employee training is essential for an organization's success. Despite the importance of training, a trainer can encounter resistance from both employees and managers. Both groups may claim that training is taking them away from their work. However, a trainer can combat this.

A growing number of employers are turning to online employee training for a hands-on, interactive way for employees to learn. More economical in both time and money than conventional training, this form of training has become more and more popular as Internet technology has improved.

Eventually, training is vital to any company. Employee training is essential for an organization's success. By implementing training program, organizations can save thousands of dollars a year. Not only will the savings pay off for your company, but you can increase productivity from your employees. Training is very much important and benefits in all hierarchical levels of the employees for improving their performance.

Inter-active computer program

As the continuous computer and high technology revolution has been affecting all the aspects of life and making plenty of difficulties around people easier, therefore, the field of management and business could get advantages in different ways to make organizations more effective and profitable to meet their supreme goals.

The reflection of the modern technology advances on management and business has been significant, as it globalized the world of business and made new opportunities and identified new untouchable markets.

One of the advantages is the advance in the field of communication and cooperation among organizations and businesses which bridges the far distances among those organizations and businesses.

The training session could increase the productivity of the company through the much needed team work.

Yes, training is a solution. A training programme can be created by using the ADDIE model.

Firstly, an assessment has to be done on what are the job related needs required by the employees to encourage team building. The assessment also must evaluate what existing knowledge participants have, and also defines the gap between what they know and what they need to know.

Secondly, Harry need to come up with a training design that meets the employees' and employer's needs. Content design, resource evaluation and a training plan needs to be drawn up. In this case, where team building and team work needs to be emphasized on, the content and learning outcomes should bring the team together.

Training development with the appropriate activities to encourage team building should be inserted into the programme. The activities could include games sessions such as a game of futsal, or solving problems in given scenarios to encourage employees to discuss amongst each other as well as provide support to their team mates. Informative motivational seminars and forums can also help build an excellent work team, and as such, should be inserted into the training programme.

Thirdly, in implementing the training programme, proper trainers should be selected to deliver the training. Trainers should be able to break the ice in any group as well as focus on the required outcome of the training programme. The trainer should also be fluent in addressing team building hiccups such as miscommunication, cold feet and lack of participation from the employees.

At the end, an evaluation needs to be conducted to see if the team responded positively to the training session, and that the training session could increase the productivity of the company through the much needed team work.

The four conditions that an organization could find useful in self-managed teams?

The first of the four conditions that an organization could find useful in self-managed teams is that the quality of work improves, the speed of work processes increase, resulting in more innovative and creative output by the organization. The better the team works together, the better the image of the organization. Secondly, greater team motivation reduces operational costs within the organization through reduction in managerial or supervisory roles. The third condition an organization could find useful would be increased efficiencies and greater employee job satisfaction resulting in increased commitment and productivity. Organization would not need to go out in search of new team member replacements every few years, spend on advertising for vacant roles and such. Lastly, the organization would experience lower turnover and absenteeism rate, which is very important and useful, as employees within the team find their roles worthwhile and job secure.

Such changes in incentive schemes will change the morale of the work force in Jirga Limited as a whole.

Thus, it is important to ensure the merit pay at JL is effective as an incentive. Firstly, the employees' participation would be a key for the successful program. Employee participation in pay-related decision is indicating employee empowerment. This is because employees able to express their concern on the new monetary pay scheme. In a reality, merit pay system often takes into account of top management perspective but neglected the view from lower management staff. In addition, employee participation also encourages transparency in merit pay performance and creates a spirit of trust and cooperation between the company and employees. However, such practice create risk where it will complicates the decision making process into a much complex process. Besides, it is also a risk where the employees involved will adverse with long term company organization.

Second suggestion would be communication. This is because not 100% employees able to participate in the decision making of the merit scheme. Therefore, communication from the top management to low management, communication between employers and employees is very important for clear message channelling. When employees know the requirement of the incentive plan, they will behave accordance to it. Employees are sensitive on the pay and it is always topics of rumours. Thus, human resource department need to choose the most suitable method for communication. Some good examples for communication are videotaped message from top management, notice, departmental meeting and others.

Thirdly, empowerment of the line managers is also a good way to ensure effective in merit pay. Line managers are the people that deal with various subordinate from different level and they often make decision on the merit pay and performance. By empowering the line manager on the merit pay, it encourages the line managers on the communication, discussion with subordinates on the scheme. In addition, empowerment also indicates that line managers are given responsible to ensure the successful of the new merit pay. He will decide the performance and reward target for the staff and he is responsible to ensure the staffs are satisfied. With performing staff, it will lead to a successful department as well.

Lastly, it is about clarity of procedure and policies. Jirga Limited need to ensure a clear procedure and policies are available to ensure the transparency and fairness on the implementation. This indicates the setting of merit, target, and procedures are being spell out clearly and documented. All staff needs to have the same procedure and approval. Any implementation with clear policies ensures there is no discrepancy in merit pay. Any discrepancy in pay will raise big response from the staff and affect the morale. Such big reaction will jeopardize the payment scheme and reputation of top management of Jirga Limited.

Mentoring programs <u>tend to be most successful when they are voluntary and participants understand details of the program. Discuss and provide ONE detailed example to support the above statement.</u>

To develop a recruitment and marketing strategy, communication is crucial in assuring a successful mentoring program. A good marketing strategy will effectively advertise the program and help recruit mentors and protégés. In addition to other challenges in communication, one of the biggest challenges of a mentoring program is recruiting mentors. Oftentimes, employees who could be potential mentors do not understand the value of participating in a mentoring program. To combat this problem, an agency's marketing strategy showcases benefits to both mentors and protégés.

Develop brochures, flyers, and posters to distribute around the agency;

• Send an email from the senior leader asking for participants;

• Post a message on the agency's intranet site advertising the program and Asking for participants;

• Conduct brown bags or career development sessions on the importance of Mentoring;

• Ask for supervisors and office chiefs to advertise the program and encourage

Participation from their employees;

• Provide agency-wide feedback regarding the value of mentoring along with Program results; and

• Provide on-going recognition of mentors.

(Department of Accounting, College of Administration and Economics/ University of Basra, Iraq)
hisham noori hussain AL-hashimy   978-1-62265-912-8 (online) 978-1-62265-913-5 (paper)

Describe THREE ways in which organizations contribute to employees' job satisfaction and retain key employees. Provide appropriate examples to support your answers.

The 3 best ways to employees' job satisfaction and retain key employees are:

Develop existing employees by offering opportunities to use skills and abilities

Give employees the opportunities to use their skills and abilities. Employees frequently have skills and abilities beyond the position for which they were hired. By developing existing employees into new roles, it is a win-win for the business and employees.

Communicate About the Total Rewards and Compensation Package

Employees rated compensation and pay as the third most important key to satisfaction. Many employees said compensation was important, but some were actually satisfied with their current compensation.

iii. Connect Employees and Senior Management

Many employees believe that good relationship with their superiors is a key to

Their satisfaction. A majority commented that communication between

Employees and senior management is important for their satisfaction. Employees value their relationship with their supervisor and senior management. An intentional two-way street can lead to increased employee satisfaction.

(Department of Accounting, College of Administration and Economics/ University of Basra, Iraq)
hisham noori hussain AL-hashimy   978-1-62265-912-8 (online) 978-1-62265-913-5 (paper)

how employers prepare managers for international assignments and for their return home. Provide an example of each point to support your answers.

In order to prepare individuals, who have been selected for an international posting, and facilitate their adjustment to the foreign culture, diverse cross-cultural training programs have been developed. The content and focus of these programs are contingent upon factors such as:

• The individual's cultural background

• Culture-specific features of the host-country environment,

• The individual's degree of contact with the host environment,

• The assignment length,

• The individual's family situation

• The individual's language skills

Repatriation presents one of the most complex sets of issues facing international human resources managers today. Successful re-entry means that the employee reaps career and personal payoffs for the overseas experience, and that the company enriches its organization through the addition of the international competencies of its repatriated employees. Repatriation difficulties vary by company, by job type and by industry. High attrition rates at re-entry, poor integration of repatriated employees, lack of appropriate positions, downsized organizations and dissatisfied repatriated employees and families are some of the most frequently cited problems. Among others, these practices included:

-Communication: the expatriate receives information and recognizes changes at home while abroad

-Validation: giving the expatriate recognition for the overseas service when this person returns home

Employees are persuaded to take foreign assignments due to several factors. Firstly, foreign or international assignment is perceived as a pre-requisite element to move forward in the management ladder. In another word, employees are willing to take up international assignment for better career

(Department of Accounting, College of Administration and Economics/ University of Basra, Iraq)
hisham noori hussain AL-hashimy   978-1-62265-912-8 (online) 978-1-62265-913-5 (paper)

advancement in the organization. For example, Lined Group, a German multinational practice such foreign assignment where executive and managerial position personnel are encourage to take up foreign assignment as part of career portfolio to move forward. Many multinational organizations have offices in countries around the world. This actually encourages the organization to have foreign assignment in order to leverage the talent within the region. For example, any technology barriers and practices in emerging market will be supported with staff from developed market. This is because the company does not need to employ a new expert into the organization. Instead, they are able to capitalize the internal talent of the company. A successful story during the foreign placement will raise the reputation of a staff and this would certainly assist during promotion exercise.

Secondly, employees are persuaded to uptake foreign assignment as a response to better remuneration package for expatriate. It is not a negative remark where reality shows that remuneration package able to motivate a person to move forward and perform better in work. As compared to local country staff, remuneration package offer to staff in foreign assignment will be much better. For example, staffs for international placement need more allowance in terms of house, insurance, taxation for them to adapt to new country easily. In addition, human resource department also will assist staff to handle their family placement, children education, even transport. Such benefit might not be provided to country local team. Furthermore, there is an opportunity to have currency gain as expatriate often been paid in mother country currency. In the event where the staff been deployed to a country which have a lower currency value, the expenses could be much lower and it also indicating a better life standard in the new country. For instance, an expatriate from England with pound sterling pay will be living much better in Malaysia using Ringgit Malaysia.

The owner and shareholders of company will benefit when company's employees are focused on making the company for profitable.

A short-term profit <u>of a month in this quarter is not conflict with long term goal provided the short-term profit is under a transparent, dignity and legal from regulations.</u>

In other word, such short-term profit must be free from ethical issues. In an organization, profit is a one of the target or long-term goal for any organization. A company will not able to sustain if running under loss or without any profit gain. Thus, profit in a month is actually contributing to long-term organization goal. Thus, under a transparent and profit reporting without discrepancies, it is not conflicting with long-term goal.

On the other hand, a short-term profit that reported without dignity and violating laws is definite conflict with long-term goal. Company is looking for long-term operation and sustainability. If any managers report short-term profit for personal interest, once the truth was revealed, this will affect the reputation of the company badly. This will lead to lost confident by customers, consumers, investors and cause the long term sustainability of the company affected. As a result, such short-team achievement is conflict with long-term goal.

<u>In the case, the goal was suspected to have discrepancy as</u> manipulation has been made to achieve short-term profit.

Managers have made changes to the financial result as a result to fulfil their personal interest. Therefore, this is against the ethical standard in any organization. Any action in organization operation should be done in-line with business ethic and policies.

However, if the short-term goal been achieved in a clean way, the goal should not be a conflict with ethical standard. Ethical standard is a guided standard on what and how a decision been made in the view of overall interest. It should not conflict with organization goal as organization goal should be achieve together with ethical standard. For example, a company should not steal intellectual properties from other company to achieve extraordinary profits as it achieves company goal, but violated ethical standard. Ethical standard did not stop company from making good profit provided an ethical way.

65

(Department of Accounting, College of Administration and Economics/ University of Basra, Iraq)
hisham noori hussain AL-hashimy   978-1-62265-912-8 (online) 978-1-62265-913-5 (paper)

There are several methods to avoid ethical and legal issues in future.

Firstly, human resource management served as recruitment and development function in an organization need to select and recruit the right person to fulfil the position. The person that selected to fulfil such managerial position must be a person with high integrity standard without any ethical issues records. On other hand, any staff that promoted internally also must have a vast reputation on the transparent attitude and behaviour. Such selection criteria can be done with reference check, 360 degree evaluation, intellectual test, balance scorecard, recommendations and other methods. A right person with high standard of clean practice will be the foundation for prevention in further ethical issues.

Secondly, ethical issue is potentially arising when there is a significant conflict of interest between shareholder and managers in organization. This is about agency problem. Thus, managers that running the company must be incentivized with different approach compared to normal staff. Human resource department need to package organization-level incentives to top management so that his personal interest is aligned to organization goals. For example, Employee Share Ownership Scheme (ESOS) can be good tools to ensure top management is working towards long term sustainability of company performance. Rather than taking into the incentive from short-term, managers will be targeting long-term goal to ensure stable share performance as they are part of shareholders.

Finally, human resource is responsible to remove staff with ethical issues. Such function must be enforced with immediate effect to give strong message to other managers where stern action is in-force. Policies and procedure can be made and communicated to all staff in organization. This will reduce the chance of manager involving in ethical issue as some managers are not preparing to put their career on stake.

Firstly, an assessment has to be done on what are the job related needs required by the employees to encourage team building. The assessment also must evaluate what existing training is a solution. A training programme can be created by using the ADDIE model.

Knowledge participants have, and also define the gap between what they know and what they need to know.

Secondly, Harry need to come up with a training design that meets the employees' and employer's needs. Content design, resource evaluation and a training plan needs to be drawn up. In this case, where team building and team work needs to be emphasized on, the content and learning outcomes should bring the team together.

Training development with the appropriate activities to encourage team building should be inserted into the programme. The activities could include games sessions such as a game of futsal, or solving problems in given scenarios to encourage employees to discuss amongst each other as well as provide support to their team mates. Informative motivational seminars and forums can also help build an excellent work team, and as such, should be inserted into the training programme.

Thirdly, in implementing the training programme, proper trainers should be selected to deliver the training. Trainers should be able to break the ice in any group as well as focus on the required outcome of the training programme. The trainer should also be fluent in addressing team building hiccups such as miscommunication, cold feet and lack of participation from the employees.

At the end, an evaluation needs to be conducted to see if the team responded positively to the training session, and that the training session could increase the productivity of the company through the much needed team work.

2. Jugra Limited (JL) is addressing the challenge to channel more of the merit -pay budget to non-management employees. Managers' merit increases are limited to 2 percent, freeing more money for everyone else. JL is urging managers to give bigger raises and bonuses to the best employees.

According to Karam Singh Wa'ia, the Chief Financial Officer this arrangement is intended to "send a signal about how you can be rewarded if you're a performer".

JL is also considering a long term-incentive plan for non-management employees. Managers already may extend the stock plan to employees who are not managers. JL develops this program and is keeping issues of fairness in mind.

Such changes in incentive schemes will change the morale of the work force in Jirga Limited as a whole. Thus, it is important to ensure the merit pay at JL is effective as an incentive. Firstly, the employees' participation would be a key for the successful program. Employee participation in pay-related decision is indicating employee empowerment. This is because employees able to express their concern on the new monetary pay scheme. In a reality, merit pay system often takes into account of top management perspective but neglected the view from lower management staff. In addition, employee participation also encourages transparency in merit pay performance and creates a spirit of trust and cooperation between the company and employees. However, such practice create risk where it will complicates the decision making process into a much complex process. Besides, it is also a risk where the employees involved will adverse with long term company organization.

Second suggestion would be communication. This is because not 100% employees able to participate in the decision making of the merit scheme. Therefore, communication from the top management to low management, communication between employers and employees is very important for clear message channelling. When employees know the requirement of the incentive plan, they will behave accordance to it. Employees are sensitive on the pay and it is always topics of rumours. Thus, human resource department need to choose the most suitable method for communication. Some good examples for communication are videotaped message from top management, notice, departmental meeting and others.

Thirdly, empowerment of the line managers is also a good way to ensure effective in merit pay. Line managers are the people that deal with various subordinate from different level and they often make decision on the merit pay and performance. By empowering the line manager on the merit pay, it encourages the line managers on the communication, discussion with subordinates on the scheme. In addition, empowerment also indicates that line managers are given responsible to ensure the successful of the new merit pay. He will decide the performance and reward target for the staff and he is responsible to ensure the staffs are satisfied. With performing staff, it will lead to a successful department as well.

Lastly, it is about clarity of procedure and policies. Jirga Limited need to ensure a clear procedure and policies are available to ensure the transparency and fairness on the implementation. This indicates the setting of merit, target, and procedures are being spell out clearly and documented. All staff needs to have the same procedure and approval. Any implementation with clear policies ensures there is no discrepancy in merit pay. Any discrepancy in pay will raise big response from the staff and affect the morale. Such big reaction will jeopardize the payment scheme and reputation of top management of Jirga Limited.

Mentoring programs <u>tend to be most successful when they are voluntary and participants understand details of the program. Discuss and provide ONE detailed example to support the above statement.</u>

To develop a recruitment and marketing strategy, communication is crucial in assuring a successful mentoring program. A good marketing strategy will effectively advertise the program and help recruit mentors and protégés. In addition to other challenges in communication, one of the biggest challenges of a mentoring program is recruiting mentors. Oftentimes, employees who could be potential mentors do not understand the value of participating in a mentoring program. To combat this problem, an agency's marketing strategy showcases benefits to both mentors and protégés.

Develop brochures, flyers, and posters to distribute around the agency;

• Send an email from the senior leader asking for participants;

• Post a message on the agency's intranet site advertising the program and Asking for participants;

• Conduct brown bags or career development sessions on the importance of Mentoring;

• Ask for supervisors and office chiefs to advertise the program and encourage

Participation from their employees;

• Provide agency-wide feedback regarding the value of mentoring along with Program results; and

• Provide on-going recognition of mentors.

1. Suka Metalbox, a manufacturing company wanted to send two senior officers for a special foreign assignment in Florida. Recently, eight employees submitted their applications to HR department and later in the two more applications reached the desk of the HR manager. Based on your HRM knowledge, explain briefly why employees are persuaded to take foreign assignments. Give appropriate examples to support your explanation.

(7 marks)

2. The owners of a corporation naturally expect the company's managers and employees to work to increase the company's value (often expressed in terms of its stock price). Other basic financial goals for a business are to increase profits through greater sales or lower costs. But can a company's people focus on those goals too much?

Consider what recently happened at Dell. An investigation by the company's audit committee found evidence of accounting adjustments over several years that appeared to be designed to show that the company had met its quarterly financial goals. These adjustments, which usually were made near the end of a quarter, shifted the timing of when income or expenses were recognized, appearing to make the company's performance better than it was. Some of the changes were approved or requested by senior executives at Dell.

The audit committee also found situations where the employees of business units gave auditors information that was incomplete or incorrect. The Securities and Exchange Commission launched an investigation to determine whether some of these actions violated the law and Dell announced to correct misinformation. The company's top management also promised to introduce controls that would prevent such manipulation of data in the future.

(Source: "Dell to Restate Earnings, Reveals Accounting Troubles" Information Week, August 16, 2007, downloaded from General Reference Center Gold, http://find galegroup.com)
Answer the following questions:

(20 marks)

2a. Who benefits when a company's employees are focused on making the company more profitable?

(1 mark)

2b. Do goals related to short-term profits –for this month of this quarter   ever conflict with longer term goals? Explain.

(6 marks)

(Department of Accounting, College of Administration and Economics/ University of Basra, Iraq)
hisham noori hussain AL-hashimy   978-1-62265-912-8 (online) 978-1-62265-913-5 (paper)

Employees are persuaded to take foreign assignments due to several factors. Firstly, foreign or international assignment is perceived as a pre-requisite element to move forward in the management ladder. In another word, employees are willing to take up international assignment for better career advancement in the organization. For example, Lined Group, a German multinational practice such foreign assignment where executive and managerial position personnel are encourage to take up foreign assignment as part of career portfolio to move forward. Many multinational organizations have offices in countries around the world. This actually encourages the organization to have foreign assignment in order to leverage the talent within the region. For example, any technology barriers and practices in emerging market will be supported with staff from developed market. This is because the company does not need to employ a new expert into the organization. Instead, they are able to capitalize the internal talent of the company. A successful story during the foreign placement will raise the reputation of a staff and this would certainly assist during promotion exercise.

Secondly, employees are persuaded to uptake foreign assignment as a response to better remuneration package for expatriate. It is not a negative remark where reality shows that remuneration package able to motivate a person to move forward and perform better in work. As compared to local country staff, remuneration package offer to staff in foreign assignment will be much better. For example, staffs for international placement need more allowance in terms of house, insurance, taxation for them to adapt to new country easily. In addition, human resource department also will assist staff to handle their family placement, children education, even transport. Such benefit might not be provided to country local team. Furthermore, there is an opportunity to have currency gain as expatriate often been paid in mother country currency. In the event where the staff been deployed to a country which have a lower currency value, the expenses could be much lower and it also indicating a better life standard in the new country. For instance, an expatriate from England with pound sterling pay will be living much better in Malaysia using Ringgit Malaysia.

The owner and shareholders of company will benefit when company's employees are focused on making the company for profitable.

A short-term profit of a month in this quarter is not conflict with long term goal provided the short-term profit is under a transparent, dignity and legal from regulations. In other word, such short-term profit must be free from ethical issues. In an organization, profit is a one of the target or long-term goal for any organization. A company will not able to sustain if running under loss or without any profit gain. Thus, profit in a month is actually contributing to long-term organization goal. Thus, under a transparent and profit reporting without discrepancies, it is not conflicting with long-term goal.

On the other hand, a short-term profit that reported without dignity and violating laws is definite conflict with long-term goal. Company is looking for long-term operation and sustainability. If any managers report short-term profit for personal interest, once the truth was revealed, this will affect the reputation of the company badly. This will lead to lost confident by customers, consumers, investors and cause the long term sustainability of the company affected. As a result, such short-team achievement is conflict with long-term goal.

In the case, the goal was suspected to have discrepancy as manipulation has been made to achieve short-term profit. Managers have made changes to the financial result as a result to fulfil their personal interest. Therefore, this is against the ethical standard in any organization. Any action in organization operation should be done in-line with business ethic and policies.

However, if the short-term goal been achieved in a clean way, the goal should not be a conflict with ethical standard. Ethical standard is a guided standard on what and how a decision been made in the view of overall interest. It should not conflict with organization goal as organization goal should be achieve together with ethical standard. For example, a company should not steal intellectual properties from other company to achieve extraordinary profits as it achieves company goal, but violated ethical standard. Ethical standard did not stop company from making good profit provided an ethical way.

There are several methods to avoid ethical and legal issues in future. Firstly, human resource management served as recruitment and development function in an organization need to select and recruit the right person to fulfil the position. The person that selected to fulfil such managerial position must be a person with high integrity standard without any ethical issues records. On other hand, any staff that promoted internally also must have a vast reputation on the transparent attitude and behaviour. Such selection criteria can be done with reference check, 360 degree evaluation, intellectual test, balance scorecard, recommendations and other methods. A right person with high standard of clean practice will be the foundation for prevention in further ethical issues.

Secondly, ethical issue is potentially arising when there is a significant conflict of interest between shareholder and managers in organization. This is about agency problem. Thus, managers that running the company must be incentivized with different approach compared to normal staff. Human resource department need to package organization-level incentives to top management so that his personal interest is aligned to organization goals. For example, Employee Share Ownership Scheme (ESOS) can be good tools to ensure top management is working towards long term sustainability of company performance. Rather than taking into the incentive from short-term, managers will be targeting long-term goal to ensure stable share performance as they are part of shareholders.

Finally, human resource is responsible to remove staff with ethical issues. Such function must be enforced with immediate effect to give strong message to other managers where stern action is in-force. Policies and procedure can be made and communicated to all staff in organization. This will reduce the chance of manager involving in ethical issue as some managers are not preparing to put their career on stake.

Question 1

The performance management helped motivate people to deliver superior performance in several ways. First, the appraisal process helped them learn just what it is that the organization considers to be ''superior.'' Second, since most employees want to be seen as superior performers, a performance appraisal process provides them with a means to demonstrate that they actually are. Finally, performance manager encouraged employees to avoid being stigmatized as inferior performers, thus meeting its strategic purpose.

The practice manager at MH has encouraged performance improvement. The performance appraisal conducted points out areas where individuals need to improve their performance. The procedure allows the organization to communicate performance expectations to every member of the team and assess exactly how well each person is doing. When everyone is clear on the expectations and knows exactly how he is performing against them, this will result in an overall improvement of the administration process.

MH is able to increase productivity and development by stressing the importance of employee personal development. Would the organization be better off sending all of its managers and professionals through a customer service training program or one on effective decision making? By reviewing the data from performance appraisals from compensation discussions, training and development professionals made good decisions about where the organization should concentrate company-wide training efforts.

Career planning points to advancement within the firm and helps the company with succession planning, reducing recruitment costs, and giving employees a stake in sticking around and making the company a success. By developing its employees, the organisation will gain better standing as it grows. In some cases though, career planning may point to a position outside the company but the relationship built may lead to reputable references for others to join the company.

The benefits would include a reduction in recruitment costs as the turnover rate decreases, better quality employees that are better equipped with the proper material and background, increase in employee loyalty that helps the company in becoming established as well as increase in productivity as the employees and the company develops together.

Question 2

The restaurant would need to be concerned that the type of disciplinary action taken against the employee is the same for all employees who misbehave against organizational rules, in this case, constantly being late for work. The risk that unfairly disciplining the employee could result in the employee retaliating, and this is counter-productive. A meeting with the said employee should be arranged to better ascertain reasons as to why the employee is always late, and if he or she encounters problems in the restaurant. Also, the organization must ensure that every employee is aware of the guidelines and consequences for breaking the rules. This could be accomplished through posting the information on the company bulletin board, in the organizational newsletter, or in employee handbooks. If an employee is always late, a reminder of the restaurant's rules and guidelines should be issued to the said employee. Should the employee still fail to abide by the rules, it will ensure that any disciplinary action taken against the employee is fair.

Every individual will have his or her own perception as to what constitutes fairness. The employee may state that it is fair that she has put in the required number of hours to cover for the late appearance. Or, it might be so that the employee, being a single parent, has issues with his sick child and is therefore allowed to be late to work.

In terms of fairness, the other employees may perceive a work rule violation as legitimate. For example, an employee arriving late to work because he has to tend to his child each day right at the shift start time, is acceptable should be fair as long as he works hard. Or, they may be unhappy about the chronically late employee having several chances to modify the behaviour because they know that another employee had been terminated after being late only once.

Question 3

Employees most frequently evaluate their pay relative to that of other employees. The workload distribution should be more or less equal in both pay wise and responsibility wise, as to that of their equal colleagues. This is to constitute an employee's idea of fairness.

Equity theory states that people measure outcomes such as pay in terms of their inputs. Employees' conclusions about equity depend upon what they choose as a standard of comparison. In this case this may be what the other employees working the different jobs are being paid for their services. The ways employees respond to their impressions about equity can have a great impact on the organization. Typically, if employees perceive equity, the employees' attitudes and behaviours continue unchanged, if they perceive an advantage, they rethink the situation to see it as merely equitable, and if the employees' perceive inequity, they are likely to make up the difference in one of three ways that include put forth less effort, find ways to increase outcomes, or by withdrawing from the organization.

Small-Business Case: Appraisals Matter at Meadow Hills (MH).

This case highlights the performance appraisal practices at MH, which has two facilities in Canada. Brian Conrad, the practice manager, conducts appraisals from compensation discussions. That way, he keeps the appraisals focused on what is getting in the way of top performance and how the employee can improve. Conrad also engages consistently with employees, and he doesn't limit his communication and feedback to problems and he doesn't limit his communication for formal appraisal meetings. These types of practices have resulted in a 10 percent turnover rate at Meadow Hills, in an industry that has a 30 percent turnover rate.

(Department of Accounting, College of Administration and Economics/ University of Basra, Iraq)
hisham noori hussain AL-hashimy   978-1-62265-912-8 (online) 978-1-62265-913-5 (paper)

CHAPTER 2

Mobile marketing

Introduction

The purpose of this report is about Mobile marketing. To identify the entire information that comprises all the mobile marketing filed, these comprises history of mobile marketing, definition of mobile marketing, top tools of mobile marketing, the mobile marketing and understand the advantages and disadvantages of mobile marketing. These are the main objectives of this report wants to provide. Therefore be we go further, we would initially begin with define the meaning of marketing. Marketing define is the process of planning and executing the conception, pricing, promotion and distribution of ideas, goods and services to create exchange that satisfy the individual and organization. Also The American Marketing Association defined: "Marketing is an organizational function and a set of processes for creating, communicating, and delivering value to customers and for managing customer relationships in ways that benefit the organization and its stakeholders". However mobile marketing is a type of marketing that involves communicating with the consumer via cellular (or mobile) device, either to send a simple marketing message, to introduce them to a new audience participation-based campaign or to allow them to visit a mobile website.

2.0 History of mobile marketing

The term 'mobile marketing' is starting to mean marketing on mobile phones or cell phones. This involves using wireless internet to broadcast advertisements and enticements for people to spend. With the spreading of hand-phone or mobile phone usage the world over, this newest major style of marketing is experiencing growth exploding.

(Department of Accounting, College of Administration and Economics/ University of Basra, Iraq)
hisham noori hussain AL-hashimy   978-1-62265-912-8 (online) 978-1-62265-913-5 (paper)

The advancement of the technology, which associated, with the development of the internet during the 1990s has moved the marketing activities to new era. During the last fifteen years, the internet as a global communication and exchange medium has witnessed huge growth. The number of created website increased from 23,000 in the year of 1995 to more 700 million website in 2014. Similarly, the online sales have grown in the same period form almost no sales in 1995 to more 1.5 trillion in 2014 (Business insiders, 2014). In United States alone, the online sales expected to reach 327 billion in 2016. Similarly, the online sales in Europe expected to reach 230 billion in 2016. The growth in the sales will be driven by the growth of mobile application and the improvement of mobile and tablet technology. In the long term, the mobile marketing is expected to surpass other traditional and non-traditional marketing methods (Internet Retailers, 2014).

The huge development of mobile technology has created a new marketing channel for marketers. Marketing through mobile devices (m-marketing) allows for innovative forms of customer relationships and is expected to lead to the development of numerous mobile commerce-based services. The mobile phone has become a "portable entertainment player, a new marketing tool for retailers and manufacturers, a multi-channel shopping device, a navigation tool, a new type of ticket and money, and a new mobile Intranet device" (Funk 2004). At the same time, the mobile phone has also become an interesting channel for transmitting advertising messages to consumers. The Wireless Advertising Association (WAA) defines wireless marketing as sending advertising messages to mobile devices such as mobile phones or PDAs through the wireless network. The use of the Short Messaging Service (SMS) to access customers through their handheld devices, in particular, has been very successful (Tsang, How, and Liang 2004). Advertisements take the form of short textual messages and are sent to customers as a form of one-to-one marketing. The rising popularity of SMS has created a new channel for mobile advertising (Bar wise and Strong 2002). In terms of the types of message sent, pull SMS advertisements are displayed to consumers who have previously indicated an interest in receiving such a message and who can then decide whether to access further information (Bruner and Kumar 2007). The world is turning to mobile and the numbers indicates that the mobile will surpass the PC in this year. There are 4 billion mobile phone in the world out of them 1.08 are smartphone and 3.05 are SMS enabled phones. Users are increasingly using their mobiles for surfing the internet. More than 50% are using their mobile for social networking activities. Mobiles are replacing PC in all fields. Statistic shows that people tend to use mobile rather than PC or webmail to open their emails. It has been found by a survey in the United States that more than 43% of the technology users use their mobile to open their emails. Only 32% open their emails using PC. In addition, webmail applications are used by 25% of the users. The use of mobile are expecting to grow and it is indicates that this technology has no replacement in the near future. Therefore, it is important for wireless advertisers to improve consumer response rates and acceptance of the advertising they received.

3.0 What is Mobile Marketing?

Definition: Mobile Marketing involves communicating with the consumer via cellular (or mobile) device, either to send a simple marketing message, to introduce them to a new audience participation-based campaign or to allow them to visit a mobile website.

Mobile Marketing is defined in many times. For instance, the Mobile Marketing Association redefined "mobile marketing" as "Mobile marketing is a set of practices that enables organizations to communicate and engage with their audience in an interactive and relevant manner through any mobile device or network." Also another definition is Mobile marketing can also be defined as "the use of the mobile medium as a means of marketing communication", the "distribution of any kind of promotional or advertising messages to customer through wireless networks". More specific definition is the following: "using interactive wireless media to provide customers with time and location sensitive, personalized information that promotes goods, services and ideas.

81

(Department of Accounting, College of Administration and Economics/ University of Basra, Iraq)
hisham noori hussain AL-hashimy   978-1-62265-912-8 (online) 978-1-62265-913-5 (paper)

Mobile marketing could be as the marketing channel utilized by any marketing collateral created for impact on a portable device. Cell phone marketing was the first premise of this arena and whilst consumers have more devices to leverage, the core principals remain the same. Marketing via cell phones at the most basic level began with SMS (Short Messaging Services). SMS advertising brought a new channel to marketers allowing them to (cautiously) target specific groups with very select campaigns. Still very effective today SMS continues as a useful opportunity. Drawbacks of SMS campaigns included the potential for higher un-subscription rates as they can be determined as very frustrating. Here is the sample picture of SMS

Figure 1: SMS advertisement by Subway

Banner advertising on web sites was the launch pad for on-line advertising the irritating banner flashing and moving at the top of websites all over the world was poised to be the saviour for advertising executives everywhere to no avail clicks dwindled as more sophisticated advertising methods came around like Google Ad Words.

Figure 2: Banner used by Sonic

Mail was an old favourite for marketing departments everywhere and its cousin e-mail marketing is now in effect a form of mobile marketing, as most email is read on mobile devices by the average consumer today. Effective marketing on mobile devices requires careful planning and delivery of e-mails via this channel. Targets do not care if the message is opened on a desktop or mobile and the message should be the same for both. Customized advertising based on reader behaviour will come to the fore. GPS enabled smart phones offer advertising based on location.

(Department of Accounting, College of Administration and Economics/ University of Basra, Iraq)
hisham noori hussain AL-hashimy   978-1-62265-912-8 (online) 978-1-62265-913-5 (paper)

Figure 3: User viewing his email from Phone

The last five years have witnessed the invention of mobile app. Using mobile app for marketing purposes have started in 2009 and it represents the first of three waves that the App is emerging through. App marketing and advertising took off early in the history of the app economy. The fermium model took place two years after. On the App Store, in-app purchase items (IAPs) were only introduced as of late 2009. On the Google Play Store, they had to wait until 2011.

Figure 4: Apps on Android

(Department of Accounting, College of Administration and Economics/ University of Basra, Iraq)
hisham noori hussain AL-hashimy   978-1-62265-912-8 (online) 978-1-62265-913-5 (paper)

(Department of Accounting, College of Administration and Economics/ University of Basra, Iraq)
hisham noori hussain AL-hashimy   978-1-62265-912-8 (online) 978-1-62265-913-5 (paper)

Since the fermium app model started making a name for it, the parameters and requirements of app advertising and user acquisition have been in constant evolution, strongly influenced by transformations of the app ecosystems. In particular, app marketers have constantly needed to adapt to the evolving policies and barriers enforced by Apple and Google.

Figure 5: App on Apple Store

(Department of Accounting, College of Administration and Economics/ University of Basra, Iraq)
hisham noori hussain AL-hashimy   978-1-62265-912-8 (online) 978-1-62265-913-5 (paper)

In fair consideration, many of the steps the two companies took were also in reaction to the evolution of advertising techniques and practices within their ecosystem. The dynamic is therefore mutual.

(Department of Accounting, College of Administration and Economics/ University of Basra, Iraq)
hisham noori hussain AL-hashimy   978-1-62265-912-8 (online) 978-1-62265-913-5 (paper)

(Department of Accounting, College of Administration and Economics/ University of Basra, Iraq)
hisham noori hussain AL-hashimy   978-1-62265-912-8 (online) 978-1-62265-913-5 (paper)

4.0 Tools of mobile Marketing

FOUR TOOLS OF MOBILE MARKETING

Apparently there are four tools of mobile marketing

4.1 text messaging / SMS

SMS is probably the most obvious tool of mobile marketing; due so many people are doing text messaging over 3 billion of people worldwide. It is only natural that this type of communication would attract marketers. The most common format of text messaging as a marketing tool is mobile couponing. Offering a discount or special offer via text message. But text messaging can and should be so much more than just coupons. Alerts, text clubs, product/service information, sending mobile site links, interactive voting, contests, text-to-donate are just a sampling of the many uses of text messaging.

4.2. Mobile-friendly websites

More than 50 million people in the US are going online with their phones and they are expecting to get websites that work on their phone. They want to find what they need quickly and easily and get back to whatever it is they were doing. The mobile web experience is not about "browsing" it is about "finding."

43. Mobile advertising

Much the same as there is banner advertising on the desktop version of the internet, there are also banner ads on mobile sites. Google made news recently by buying ad mob, one of the leading mobile display ad networks, and it is safe to say that mobile display (or banner) advertising will be a much more used tool in marketing now.

Additionally there is pay per click advertising which is aligned with mobile search. A consumer searching for something their phone will see search results ads showing along with the organic listings they find. Naturally, Google is a huge player in this space as well with their Google mobile ad words program.

4.4 mobile emails

Each day millions of people check their email on their phone. Whether the businesses sending emails to these people intended to be mobile marketing or not, they most certainly are. Once a person is communicating and engaging with you on their mobile device you are doing mobile marketing. Every email that is sent must be easily readable on a mobile device or become so within one click. People are deluged by email and it is not likely that they will look at your email twice. If the first opportunity to see it comes on their mobile, it darn well better work because you will not get a second chance when they are on their desktop later.

5.0 Type of Mobile Marketing

There are many types of mobile marketing that have been used and still being used by marketers to promote their products and services. Figure shows the types of these mobile marketing tools and detailed explanation of the tools follow in the next subsections.

(Department of Accounting, College of Administration and Economics/ University of Basra, Iraq)
hisham noori hussain AL-hashimy   978-1-62265-912-8 (online) 978-1-62265-913-5 (paper)

(Department of Accounting, College of Administration and Economics/ University of Basra, Iraq)
hisham noori hussain AL-hashimy   978-1-62265-912-8 (online) 978-1-62265-913-5 (paper)

5.1 Short Messaging Service Marketing

Marketing through cell phones' SMS became increasingly popular in the early 2000s in Europe and some parts of Asia when businesses started to collect mobile phone numbers and send off wanted (or unwanted) content. On average, SMS messages are read within four minutes, making them convertible. Over the past few years, SMS marketing has become a legitimate advertising channel in some parts of the world. This is because unlike email over the public internet, the carriers who policy their own networks have set guidelines and best practices for the mobile media industry including mobile advertising. The Mobile Marketing Association has established guidelines and is evangelizing the use of the mobile channel for marketers. While this has been successful in developed regions such as North America, Western Europe and some other countries, mobile SPAM messages (SMS sent to mobile subscribers without a legitimate and explicit opt-in by the subscriber) remain an issue in many other parts or the world, partly due to the carriers selling their member databases to third parties. Mobile marketing via SMS has expanded rapidly in Europe and Asia as a new channel to reach the consumer. SMS initially received negative media coverage in many parts of Europe for being a new form of spam as some advertisers purchased lists and sent unsolicited content to consumer's phones; however, as guidelines are put in place by the mobile operators, SMS has become the most popular branch of the Mobile Marketing industry with several 100 million advertising SMS sent out every month in Europe alone. In Europe, the first cross-carrier SMS short code campaign was run by Txtbomb in 2001 for an Island Records release, In North America it was the Labatt Brewing Company in 2002. Over the past few years, mobile short codes have been increasingly popular as a new channel to communicate to the mobile consumer. Brands have begun to treat the mobile short code as a mobile domain name allowing the consumer to text message the brand at an event, in store and off any traditional media. SMS marketing services typically run off a short code, but sending text messages to an email address is another methodology. Short codes are 5 or 6 digit numbers that have been

91

assigned by all the mobile operators in a given country for the use of brand campaign and other consumer services. Due to the high price of short codes of \$500–\$1000 a month, many small businesses opt to share a short code in order to reduce monthly costs. The mobile operators vet every short code application before provisioning and monitor the service to make sure it does not diverge from its original service description. Another alternative to sending messages by short code or email is to do so through one's own dedicated phone number.

Besides short codes, inbound SMS can be received on long numbers (international number format, e.g. +44 7624 805000 or US number format, e.g. 757 772 8555), which can be used in place of short codes or premium-rated short messages for SMS reception in several applications, such as product promotions and campaigns. Long numbers are internationally available, as well as enabling businesses to have their own number, rather than short codes, which are usually shared across a number of brands. Additionally, long numbers are non-premium inbound numbers.

One key criterion for provisioning is that the consumer opts into the service. The mobile operators demand a double opt in from the consumer and the ability for the consumer to opt out of the service at any time by sending the word STOP via SMS. These guidelines are established in the CTIA Playbook and the MMA Consumer Best Practices Guidelines, which are followed by all mobile marketers in the United States. In Canada, opt in will be mandatory once the Fighting Internet and Wireless Spam Act comes in force in mid-2012.

(Department of Accounting, College of Administration and Economics/ University of Basra, Iraq)
hisham noori hussain AL-hashimy   978-1-62265-912-8 (online) 978-1-62265-913-5 (paper)

5.2 Multimedia Message Service

Multimedia Message Service mobile marketing can contain a timed slideshow of images, text, audio, and video. This mobile content is delivered via <u>MMS</u> (Multimedia Message Service). Nearly all new phones produced with a color screen are capable of sending and receiving standard MMS message. Brands are able to both send (mobile terminated) and receive (mobile originated) rich content through MMS A2P (application-to-person) mobile networks to mobile subscribers. In some networks, brands are also able to sponsor messages that are sent P2P (person-to-person).

Good examples of mobile-originated MMS marketing campaigns are Motorola's on-going campaigns at House of Blues venues, where the brand allows the consumer to send their mobile photos to the LED board in real-time as well as blog their images online.

5.3 Push Notifications

Push notifications were first introduced to smartphones by Apple with the advent of the iPhone in 2007. They were later further popularized with the Android operational system, where the notifications are shown on the top of the screen. It has helped application owners to communicate directly with their end users in a simple and effective way. If not used wisely it can quickly alienate users as it causes interruptions to their current activities on the phone. It can be much cheaper if compared to SMS marketing for the

93

long run, but it can become quite expensive on the short run, because the cost involved in application development. Once the application is downloading and installed provided the feature is not turned off it is practically free, because it uses internet bandwidth only. SMS and push notifications can be part of a well-developed inbound mobile marketing strategy.

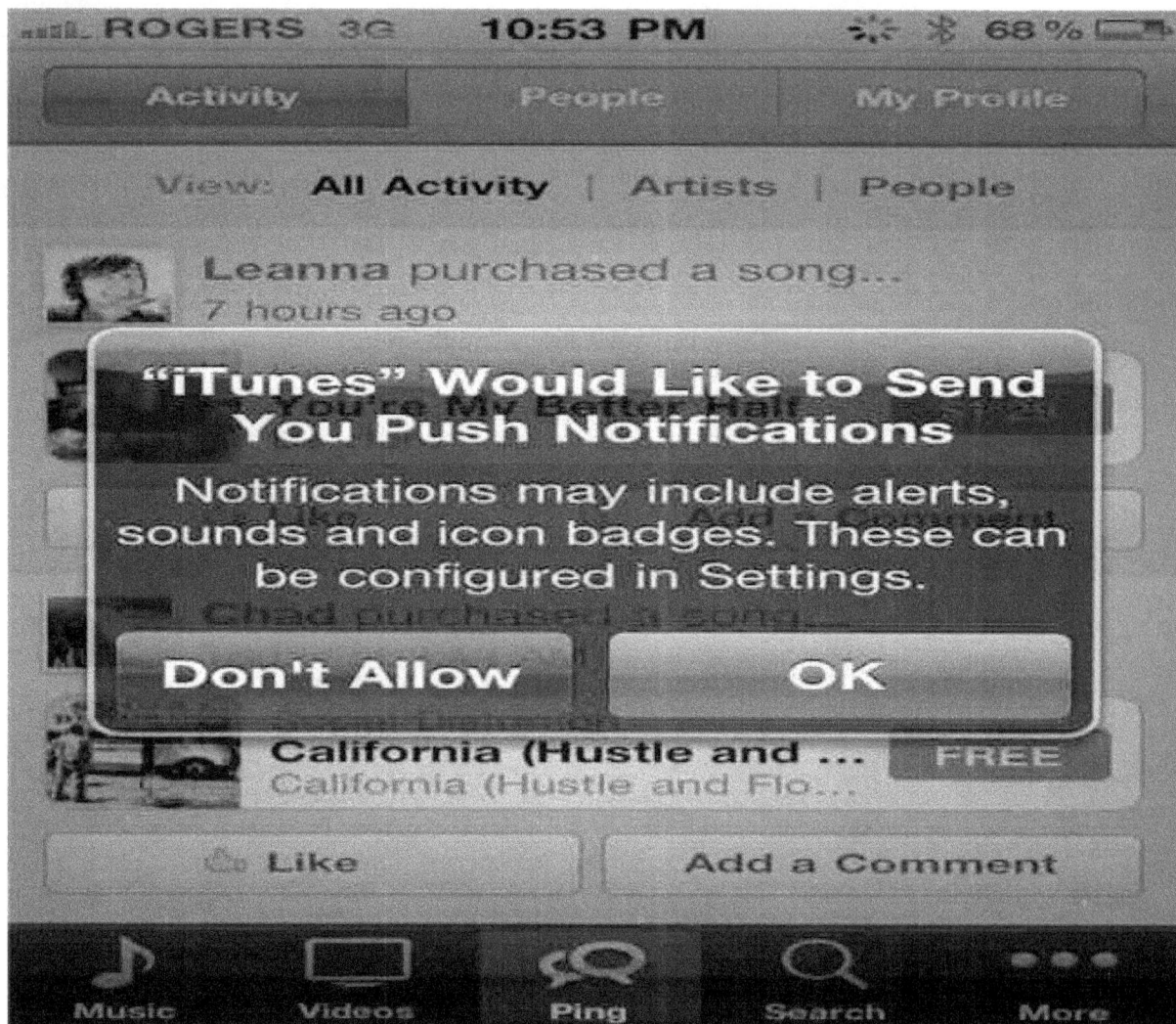

5.4 App-based Marketing

With the increasingly widespread use of smartphones, app usage has also greatly increased. Therefore, mobile marketers have increasingly taken advantage of smartphone apps as a marketing resource. This allows for direct engagement, payment, and targeted advertising. Further description of App-based application was given above in the history of mobile marketing. The picture below is shown the example of mobile marketing applications.

4.5 In-Game Mobile Marketing

There are essentially four major trends in mobile gaming right now: interactive real-time 3D games, massive multi-player games, and social networking games. Real-time 3d game is kind of game that normally referred to the movie or novel that have been made. This kind of game is showing exactly as real person, environment in the game like a reality. Mobile marketer are using this method to post advertising of different kind of product like billboard sign in the game, to attract the consumer, they also use racing games with different sort of car brand that would attract customers. The picture is below is showing real-time 3d games on mobile phone and tablets.

(Department of Accounting, College of Administration and Economics/ University of Basra, Iraq)
hisham noori hussain AL-hashimy   978-1-62265-912-8 (online) 978-1-62265-913-5 (paper)

Social network games are amongst the most popular games played in the world, with several products with tens of millions of players. It's a type of online game that is played through social networks, and typically features multiplayer and asynchronous gameplay mechanics. Social network games are most often implemented as browser games, but can also be implemented on other platforms such as mobile devices. With the invention of smartphone devices, social games have now also seen widespread adoption on mobile platforms such as is and Android devices. The picture below is shown the example   of   social   networking   game   on   mobile   phone

On the other side, there are also casual games, for example games that are very simple and very easy to play. Most mobile games today are such casual games and this will probably stay so for quite a while to come. Brands are now delivering promotional messages within mobile games or sponsoring entire games to drive consumer engagement. This is known as mobile advert-gaming or Ad-funded mobile game.

5.6 Mobile Web Marketing

Advertising on web pages specifically meant for access by mobile devices is also an option. The Mobile Marketing Association provides a set of guidelines and standards that give the recommended format of ads, presentation, and metrics used in reporting. Google, Yahoo, and other major mobile content providers have been selling advertising placement on their properties for years already as of the time of this writing. Advertising networks focused on mobile properties, SMS resellers and advertisers are available. Additionally, web forms on web pages can be used to integrate with mobile texting sources for reminders about meetings, seminars and other important events that assume users are not always at their computers. In addition Mobile websites are another aspect of mobile web marketing and can be a tool than can used to help make purchasing goods and services easier as well as create better communication opportunities between trades.

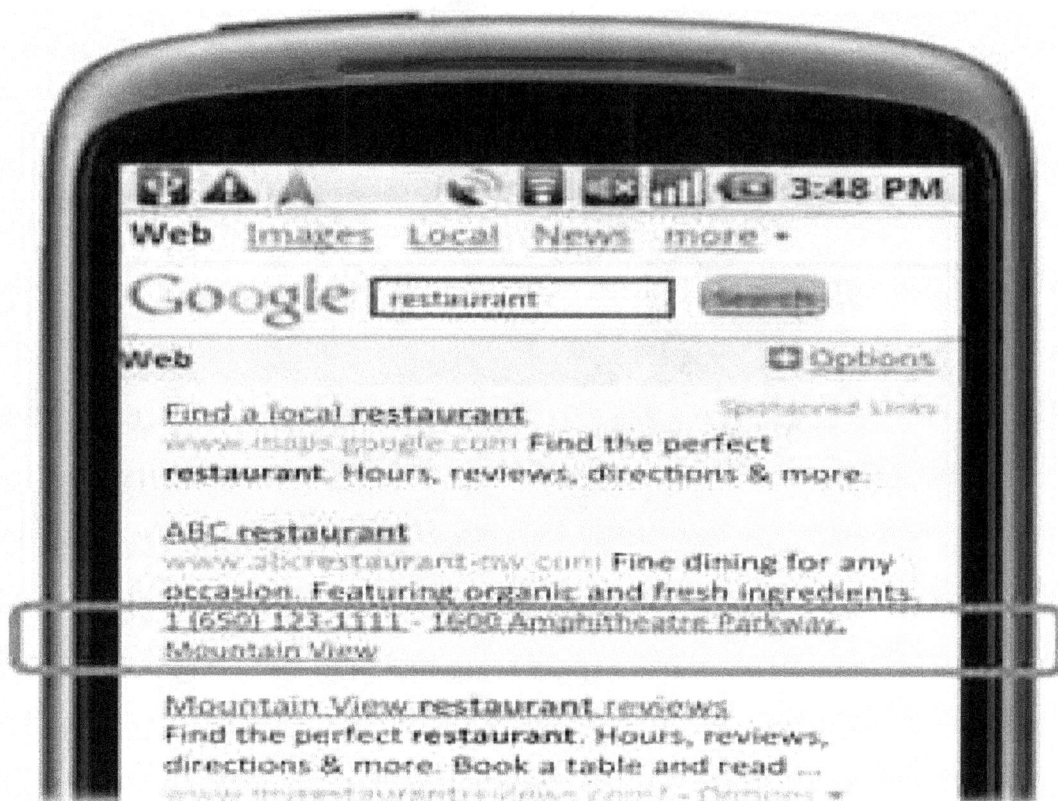

5.7 QR Codes

QR codes would allow a customer to visit a web page address by scanning a 2D image with their phone's camera, instead of manually entering a URL. The resultant URLs typically includes tracking features, which would be heavy of unwieldy if typed by the customer. Originally approved as an ISS standard in 1997, Denso-Wave first developed the standard for tracking automobile parts in Japan. QR codes have been growing in popularity in Asia and Europe, but have been slow to be adopted in North America. Some high-profile QR campaigns in the United States have included billboards by Calvin Klein in Times Square, QR codes for every SKU in Home Depot and Best Buy stores, and a scavenger hunt promoting Starbucks. The picture below is shown the QR code of Starbucks.

Apple Passbook (application), implemented as a native app for iOS6, has employed QR codes as one of the ways that the iPhone (or iPod Touch) users can take a real world action. For example, scan the Barcode on their Passbook Pass. In addition to QR codes, the Passbook (application) also supports PDF417 and Aztec 2D Barcodes

5.8 Bluetooth

The growth of Bluetooth began around 2003 and a few companies in Europe have started establishing successful businesses. Most of these businesses offer "hotspot" systems, which comprise of some kind of content-management system with a Bluetooth distribution function. This technology has the advantages that it is permission-based, has higher transfer speeds and is a radio-based technology and can therefore not be billed (i.e. is free of charge). The likely earliest device built for mobile marketing via Bluetooth was the context tag of the AmbieSense project (2001-2004). More recently, Tata Motors conducted one of the biggest Bluetooth marketing campaigns in India for its brand the Sumo Grande and more of such activities have happened for brands like Walt Disney promoting their movie 'High School Musical'

5.9 Infrared

Infrared is the oldest and most limited form of mobile marketing. Some European companies have experimented with "shopping window marketing" via free Infrared waves in the late 1990s. However, infrared has a very limited range (approx. 10 cm - 1meter) and could never really establish itself as a leading Mobile Marketing technology.

5.10 Proximity systems

Mobile marketing via proximity systems, or proximity marketing, relies on GSM 03.41, which defines the Short Message Service - Cell Broadcast. SMS-CB allows messages (such as advertising or public information) to be broadcast to all mobile users in a specified geographical area. In the Philippines, GSM-based proximity broadcast systems are used by select Government Agencies for information dissemination on Government-run community-based programs to take advantage of its reach and popularity. It is also used for commercial service known as Proximal SMS. Blue water, a super-regional shopping Centre in the UK, has a GSM based system supplied by NTL to help its GSM coverage for calls, it also allows each customer with a mobile phone to be tracked though the Centre which shops

(Department of Accounting, College of Administration and Economics/ University of Basra, Iraq)
hisham noori hussain AL-hashimy   978-1-62265-912-8 (online) 978-1-62265-913-5 (paper)

they go into and for how long. The system enables special offer texts to be sent to the phone. For example, a retailer could send a mobile text message to those customers in their database who have opted-in, who happen to be walking in a mall. That message could say "Save 50% in the next 5 minutes only when you purchase from our store."

5.11 Location-based services

Location-based services (LBS) are offered by some cell phone networks as a way to send custom advertising and other information to cell-phone subscribers based on their current location. The cell-phone service provider gets the location from a global positioning system GPS chip built into the phone, or using radiolocation and trilateration based on the signal-strength of the closest cell-phone towers (for phones without GPS features). In the United Kingdom, which launched location-based services in 2003, networks do not use trilateration; LBS services use a single base station, with a 'radius' of inaccuracy, to determine a phone's location. Some location-based services work without GPS tracking technique, instead transmitting content between devices peer-to-peer.

5.12 User-controlled Media

Mobile marketing differs from most other forms of marketing communication in that it is often user (consumer) initiated (mobile originated) message, and requires the express consent of the consumer to receive future communications. A call delivered from a server (business) to a user (consumer) is called a mobile terminated (MT) message. This infrastructure points to a trend set by mobile marketing of consumer controlled marketing communications.

Due to the demands for more user-controlled media, mobile messaging infrastructure providers have responded by developing architectures that offer applications to operators with more freedom for the users, as opposed to the network-controlled media. Along with these advances to user-controlled Mobile Messaging 2.0, blog events throughout the world have been implemented in order to launch popularity in the latest advances in mobile technology. In June 2007, Air wide Solutions became the official sponsor for the Mobile Messaging 2.0 blog that provides the opinions of many through the discussion of mobility with freedom.

6.0 Features of Mobile Marketing

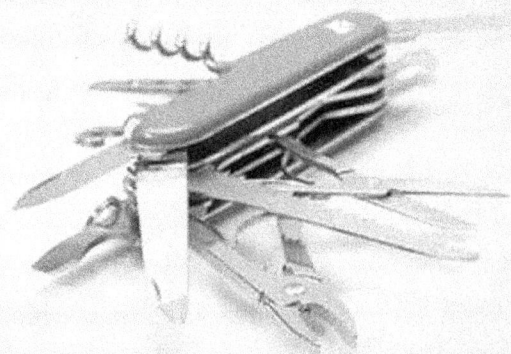

Mobile Marketing Features

There are many characteristic that mobile phone is characterized with comparing with other tools. Mobile is always with us wherever we go. It is handily portable, small size and ease to be used. With direct response and relatively lower cost of communication, mobile is changing the face of the marketing and advertising horizon. According to Atone (2008) has identified seven features unique to mobile phones, highlighting the unique benefits and challenges of the mobile phone.

6.1 The Mobile Phone is Personal

The result of survey conducted by marketing association found that more than 63% of the respondents do not prefer to share their phone with anyone else. The percentage was higher in japan where 90% of the respondents mention that their phone is very personal and no one shall have it in his hand. While laptops do present a personal connection to the Internet, they are not as personal a device as the mobile phone.

From mobile marketing point view, marketers must respect the privacy of users and they must have permission is exceptionally important in all aspects of marketing, and particularly so when it comes to mobile phones.

6.2 The Mobile Phone is Always Carried

Mobile has become essential part of the things that a normal man carries out when he go anywhere. Furthermore, the mobile sleeps near the owner in most cases. According to 2007 research by Morgan Stanley, 91% of mobile phone owners keep their phone within one meter, 24 hours a day. People have their phones with them at all times of the day, even in the bathroom. Messages sent to recipients can be read and acted on immediately. Unlike, for example, email, which requires that the recipient be in front of their computer and connected to the Internet, messages sent to mobile phones will most likely, be accessed within minutes of being received.

6.3 The Mobile Phone is always on

In order to fulfil its primary function – as a telephone – the mobile phone is always on. Messages and services can be sent and acted on at all times of the

(Department of Accounting, College of Administration and Economics/ University of Basra, Iraq)
hisham noori hussain AL-hashimy   978-1-62265-912-8 (online) 978-1-62265-913-5 (paper)

day. Similar to the previous feature of the phone, the fact that the phone is always on changes the services and messages that can be developed for the phone. It also means that marketers need to be even more sensitive with their marketing communications. Not many people would appreciate an SMS at 4am informing them of a special offer.

6.4 The Mobile Phone has a Built-In Payment System

This is perhaps the key feature of the mobile phone, and one reason why content for mobile phones in many areas generates as much or more revenue than content for the Internet. Every mobile phone has a built in payment mechanism – the SIM card. Billing is easily handled through the user's mobile network. Not only do mobile phones have this built-in payment mechanism, paying for content and downloads has been built into the way that consumers use their phones. There is less of an expectation that goods and services will be free.

There are also a number of services that turn the mobile into a virtual wallet or bankcard, bringing banking and payment services to people all around the world. Channel, a mobile news ticker feed in Japan, generates US$ 192 million per year in subscriptions for its US$ 2 a month service. It has more paying subscribers on this single service that all online newspapers in the world combined (Moore, 2008). Similar cases can be made for games, music, and other mobile content. Consumers are willing to pay for services and content on their mobile. Advertising is not the only way to generate revenue for content.

6.5 Availability at the Point of Creative Inspiration

As the mobile phone is always carried and always on, it is always available as a creative tool. Phones today feature a number of tools that let users act on creative impulse, from taking photos and videos, to becoming a scribbling pad on which to jot down ideas. The feature can be used to encourage

104

interactivity within campaigns created for mobile. It presents the mobile as a useful tool in viral campaigns based on consumer-generated content.

6.6 Accurate Audience Measurement

While the Internet is hugely superior to other media in its ability to track and measure advertising and marketing campaigns, it is hidden by the mobile phone. Every transaction made on a mobile phone can be uniquely tracked to that mobile phone number, whether the transaction is a voice call, an SMS message, or accessing the Internet. Aggregated data provides extensive profiling and segmenting opportunities for targeting the right audience. Campaigns can also be accurately measured and tracked for ROI. This accurate measurement means that mobile phone users have far less anonymity than Internet users.

6.7 Capturing the Social Context of Media Consumption

This represents emerging thinking on the benefits of the mobile. Because of the nature of the mobile phone to accurately track transactions to any particular phone number (user), it can track transactions between mobile numbers (users). This means that sophisticated data mining can identify patterns that indicate information and preferences of mobile phone users. Not only can alpha users be identified, but also they may be identified within their social context. This information will represent rich data that can be used to both create and market products, content and services online.

7.0 Advantages of Mobile Marketing

There was a time when e-Marketing was very much the thing for all marketers. Offering various benefits, it had practically changed the face of conventional marketing and the way companies viewed this aspect of business. Now, with the further arrival of advanced mobile devices bringing in a lot more connectivity, Mobile Marketing is going far beyond e-Marketing. Mobile marketing gives the user more advantages, such as lower cost, customization, easy tracking and so on, thereby reducing work force and yet giving the entrepreneur better business benefits and profits. In this section, briefly the benefits of mobile marketing for marketers are discussed.

7.1 Cost

Mobile advertising costs a fraction of what television and radio ads cost. Creating content such as images or video for streamlined mobile devices is relatively inexpensive when compared to desktop or laptop systems, which can handle content of the highest quality. The limitations of mobile devices such as screen sizes, data transfer rates and costs mean that content needs to be simple when created for mobile. This mobile efficiency is also great for promotions, issuing vouchers and other permission-based marketing and incentive services. Promotional codes and coupons can be relayed to the audience via mobile devices, allowing users to 'carry' around the virtual information and use at a convenient time.

7.2 Easy to work with

Drawing out content for mobile devices, whether it is text, images or video is simpler and less expensive as compared with the same for desktops or laptops. The mobile medium also makes easier to issue promotions and marketing incentive services to the user. Furthermore, the user can keep the virtual information with him and carry it around until the time he needs to use it.

7.3 Mass communication made easy

Today a lot more people own mobile phones than desktops or laptops; mobile marketing helps the marketer reach a far wider and diverse audience, especially in the more remote regions of the world. Mobile marketing also gives the entrepreneur the advantage of geo-location and sending location-specific messages to users, using GPS and Bluetooth technology.

Mobile Marketing is often able to reach a wider audience due to the accessibility of mobile devices when compared to the number of those who have access to traditional, desktop-based Internet, especially in developing countries such as South Africa. There is often potential for device detection, geo-locating, location-based messaging (such as location specific and sales related broadcasting Bluetooth messages in shopping center) and other handy tools for targeting.

7.3 Mobile payment

The latest mobile payment facility is very convenient for the users today. Here, users are offered a secure online payment environment, which works via advanced mobile Web systems. This means that the user does not need to use physical currency each time he wants to make a mobile purchase or pay a bill online.

7.4 Instant results

People always carry their mobile phones with them. Most of the time, the user has his mobile phone on as well, which means, he or she receives the message at the very moment it is sent. Even if it is in standby mode, the message is received as soon as the user turns on his mobile device. For this reason, mobile marketing techniques are always almost instant.

7.5 Tracking user response

User response can be tracked almost straightaway. This helps the mobile marketer better understand and analyse user behaviour, thus improving their own standards of service.

7.6 Micro blogging benefits

Mobile users are increasingly using micro blogging platforms like Twitter from their mobile phones. This micro blogging feature can be very highly beneficial to the marketer. Because today almost every company has blog like twitter. Which they can post news, new product, or any upcoming events for their customer.

8.0 Disadvantages of Mobile Marketing

Similar to any other tools, mobile marketing has its own disadvantages. These disadvantages are:

8.1 Privacy and Permission

One of the major problems in mobile marketing is privacy protection. So in this case Mobile marketers need to understand and respect the fact that users would like their privacy online. So they should only indulge in promotional activity if they have the user's permission for it.

8.2 Platforms too different

Mobile devices do not have any particular standard, as compared to PCs and laptops. Mobile phones come in many shapes and sizes, so screen size is never constant. Besides, mobile platforms very differ from each other, using different OS' and browsers. Hence creating one campaign for all of them can get difficult.

8.3 Navigation on a Mobile Phone

The mobile phone usually comes with a small screen and no mouse. This means that navigation on a mobile phone may get difficult for the user, even if it has a touchscreen. In such a case, most ads may go untouched, as the user may find it too tedious to look in detail through each one of them.

9.0 Strategies and Recommendation for Mobile Marketing

There are several strategies that mobile marketers need to consider; therefore the following recommendation and strategies are suggested to the marketers to increase the effectiveness of mobile marketing.

9.1 Integrate with social media

According to First Data, an online payment system provider, 81 present of smartphone users check social media to read reviews before making a purchase. Marketers who have integrated their mobile program with customer reviews and social media sharing buttons for Facebook, Twitter, and Interest are reaping the rewards. Amazon and Betsy are two examples.

There is a new business model emerging, it is mixing social media with e-commerce, and it is called social commerce. The growth of this business model is dramatic therefore; marketer must integrate and enter the social media to reap the benefits.

9. 2 Timing

Timing is everything for mobile. Marketers who send notifications too early in the morning or during dinner will only annoy subscribers. Let customers set their own parameters for when and how they are contacted via SMS alerts or push notifications. Integra, for example, allows users to customize the types of notifications they want to receive via push.

9.3 Raise awareness when timing is everything

The average user looks at their mobile phone up to 150 times a day, making mobile a vital channel to raise brand awareness. Online shopping sites will provide their subscribers with push notifications every day at 11am to update them on the latest flash sales.

9.4 Deliver coupons via SMS

Increasingly, marketers consider mobile as the most relevant engagement channel, which is no surprise since four out of five consumers now use their smartphones to shop. Marketers who want to raise awareness for special offers send coupons via SMS or push notifications.

9.5 Analyse customer data

Consumers view their mobile devices, as more personal than their email or web browser, so be relevant and respectful. Use location, age, demographic and other information to segment subscribers and to send them relevant and timely content.

10.0 The future of mobile marketing

As the world of technology is evolving, mobile is one of the most innovative technology platforms out today, and with about 50% of mobile users owning a smartphone, the market for apps and further technological advancement is greater now than ever before. The future of mobile marketing actually started already. Therefore these are the few future of mobile marketing.

10.1 Create experiences and influence purchases

The Internet already makes smartphone users' lives easier, but the key is fine-tuning what it has already done to make things more efficient. Mobile devices have come a long way, but there is a lot more advancement to come. This could include being able to order pictures directly from a mobile device's photo album or scanning a piece of furniture's barcode to find a tutorial about how to assemble it. With almost every electronic device being able to connect to the Internet, advancement will only continue.

10.2 Facilitating Experiences

Foursquare and Yelp have released app updates recently that allow users to be notified when their friends have checked into the same location or are nearby. This type of GPS-location for a user's social network is even further reducing the need to communicate directly with friends to find out where they are. This can be useful when attending large events, going out with new friends while running into some new ones or even avoiding an ex-girlfriend/boyfriend/husband/wife or boss. Besides utilizing mobile to market locations as a place where a user's friends are hanging out, mobile apps can also be used to market events or unique experiences. This includes secret concerts or performances for only certain app users or a special on hot air balloon rides that a user just happens to be a few blocks away from. Users like the gratification of having apps do the work for them. That way, they can focus more on their friends and the experience itself, rather than spending effort having to find it.

10.3 Comparing prices

Mobile devices already make it easy for users to check prices of products and services as well as look for coupons and discounts. This will only advance as well. In the future, a restaurant could pick up a negative tweet about a competitor and instantly send them a coupon. The possibilities are endless.

10.4 Mobile redefining customer service.

Social networks are becoming a huge resource for customers to post their comments, questions and complaints. One in five consumers' uses social media sites to have their voices heard. In the future, this number is expected to skyrocket and for customer service via social media to be the norm for businesses. While mobile marketing has already come quite far in just the past few years, the fact remains that there is much more that can still be done. With almost every electronic device available being built to connect to the Internet, smartphones and other gadgets alike will bring marketers and users together to create experiences, influence purchases and make life a little easier. The picture below is shown how mobile phone and tablet are leaving pc and desktop behind in the future.

(Department of Accounting, College of Administration and Economics/ University of Basra, Iraq)
hisham noori hussain AL-hashimy   978-1-62265-912-8 (online) 978-1-62265-913-5 (paper)

Conclusion

From the information above had identified the definition of mobile marketing, the top tools and types of mobile marketing, brief history of mobile marketing and how it's evolving rapidly now and in the future and also the features, advantages and disadvantages of mobile marketing. The information above has shown what tremendous opportunities in the mobile marketing are, the Mobile marketing is an effective ways of attracting customers. The emerging facts refer to the growing of the market of mobile. In 2014, it is expected that the mobile will surpass the desktop or laptop use. Marketers have to consider the benefits of mobile marketing and capitalize on these benefits and try to minimize and reduce the drawbacks of the mobile marketing by choosing the right message and sending it in the right time to the right customers.

CHAPTER 3

Some rules of low

<u>Five</u> rights of agents <u>and explain each one for this right how become duties for the principals.</u>

1. Right to remuneration

One of the rights of agents is remuneration as the principal have the duty to remunerate the agent. This occurs when the agent has been instrument in the occurrence of the event which the principal agreed to remunerate the agent for. It must be noted that this duty only arises when the agent earns it. The case of Green v. Bartlett illustrated how an agent was not entitled to commission on the sale when the buyer purchased without the agent's intervention. This was despite that the said buyer learnt of the owner through the agent he met at auction earlier. The principal is only liable to pay remuneration to agent when the agent has performed what he expressly contracted to do or in the event that the principal has wrongfully revoked his agent's authority or otherwise interfered with his performance of the undertaking.

2.   Right   to   indemnity

the other right of agents is the principal owes the duty to indemnify the agent against losses, liabilities and expenses incurred in the performance of the undertaking. This obligation maybe expressly stated in the contract or implied as the extent of this liability depends upon the nature of the agreement between the parties and the kind of business the agent is employed to undertake. However, the principal has no such obligation when the agent has acted unlawfully.

3. Right of lien

Another right of the agents is the right of lien when the agent who is in lawful of possession of goods or chattels belonging to principal has the right to retain possession of them until payment by the principle of agreed

113

remuneration or reimbursement of the agent's reasonable expenses. This right exists only if the goods or chattels have been lawfully obtained by the agent in the course of the agency and that such goods or chattels have not been delivered to the agent with express directions or for a special purpose. An example of this is when the principal delivers an equipment to the agent with the express instruction that he deliver that item to a third party; the agent is not entitled to claim a lien on the equipment.

4.   Right   to   compensation

the agent also has the right to compensation as the principal is liable to pay compensation for the injuries sustained by the agent due to principal's negligence or lack of skill. However, it is also clear that the principal has no obligation to pay compensation to the agent when the agent himself causes injuries to himself due to his own negligence.

5. Right to cooperation

Finally, the agent has the right to cooperation as the principal has the obligation to provide cooperation and assistance to the agent in performing his duties. In other words, the principal must do nothing to prevent the performance of the agent in carrying out his work as employed.

Five rights of principals and explain each one for this right how become duties for the agents.

1. Right to agent's performance of the contract

The first right of the principals is the agent owes the duty to perform what he has undertaken to do as contracted especially when the agency is contractual. Chiefly, this involves carrying out and performing the contract. The case of Turpin v. Belton highlights that the failure of an agent under the contract to insure the principal's ship caused him to be seen as breaching the contract. However, the non-performance of the contract is allowed when the agent is contracted to perform the undertaking that is illegal or null and void by common   law   and   statute.

2. Right to agent's action in accordance with the authority and duties as imposed by contract

Another right of the principals is the agent must act in accordance with the authority and duties imposed on him by the contract. The failure of an agent to do so will mean that the agent will be liable in damages for breach of contract and his right to remuneration will be forfeited as well. In the case of Fraser v. BR Furman (Production) Ltd Insurance Brokers, the defendant agreed to affect the plaintiff's liability policy for a consideration but failed to do so. As a result, the defendant was held liable for damages and succeeded in claiming indemnity from the broker.

3. Right to agent's duty to account

The other right of the principals is the agent must pay all his money to his principal received to the use of his principal. In short, this is known as the duty to account. Such obligation exists even if the transaction in respect of which the money is received by the agent on behalf of the principal sold or illegal as long as the contract of the agent itself is not illegal. For the proper performance, this duty requires the agent to be in the position to know what he must pay.

4. Right to agent's duty not to make secret profit

In addition, another right that is entitled to the principals is that the agent has the duty not to make secret profit. The agent must not accept a bribe or secret commission as these are the things that show that the agent has put himself in a position where such a conflict of interest might cause the agent to act against the principal's interests.

5. Right to agent's duty to act in good faith

finally, the agent has the duty to act in good faith as the principal is entitled to this right. This duty to act in good faith means that the agent must not allow his duty and personal interest to conflict. In other words, the agent has to make sure that he has acted honestly, fairly and openly in his dealings with his principal. Hence, it is important for an agent to be acting in good faith in all of his dealings as this is a right and entitlement of the principal in a smooth relationship between an agent and the principal.

What is the jurisdiction of courts? Jurisdiction of the courts relates to the power of courts to adjudicate cases and issue orders. Basically, the jurisdiction of courts in Malaysia usually has the power to hear either civil or criminal cases according to Subordinate Courts Act 1948 and the Courts of Judicature Act 1964. The jurisdiction of the courts in Malaysia is divided between Superior courts (Federal Court, Court of Appeal and High Court) and Subordinate courts (Sessions Court and Magistrates' Court).

While all of these courts can hear criminal or civil cases, the jurisdiction of these courts shows that each of them have differing powers in hearing types of cases, deciding the sentences and power to hear appeals. Article 121 of the Federal Constitution of Malaysia establishes two High Courts of parallel jurisdiction and they are High Court of Malaya and High Court of Sabah and Sarawak. In other words, one High Court covers the area of Peninsular Malaysia while another covers the area of Sabah and Sarawak.

Distinguish the jurisdiction of these three courts (Federal Courts, Court of Appeal, and High Court).

Federal   *Court*

There is four main jurisdictions that are enforced within the Malaysian Federal Court, which are the Exclusive Jurisdiction, Referral Jurisdiction, Advisory Jurisdiction, and Hearing and Determining Appeals.

The Exclusive Jurisdiction determines whether a law made by Parliament or by the State Legislature is invalid or not, and to resolve the issues that arise between States, or between the Federation with any State. This jurisdiction is provided in Article 128(1) of the Malaysian Federal Constitution.

Referral Jurisdiction on the other hand determines any questions that arise in the hearing of other courts to the effect of any provision of the Federal Constitution, and send the base back to that court to be decided according to the determination. This is done without interfering the jurisdiction of the Federal Court, and to hear and determine appeals and subject to any rules of court regulating the exercise of that jurisdiction. This jurisdiction is provided in Article 128(2) of the Malaysian Federal Constitution.

The third jurisdiction of the Federal Court in Malaysia would be the Advisory Jurisdiction. The Yang Di-Pertain Aging may refer to the Federal Court for its opinion on any question regarding the Federal Constitution or any other constitutional issues. The opinion of the Federal Court shall be pronounced in an open court. This jurisdiction is provided in Article 130 of the Malaysian Federal Constitution.

The fourth and final jurisdiction of the Federal Court would be the Hearing and Determining Appeals. These appeals could either be civil or criminal appeals. The Federal Court may hear and determine appeals against decisions of the Court of Appeal to any criminal matter decided by the High Court in the exercise of its original jurisdiction. This jurisdiction is provided in the section 87 in the Courts of Judicature Act 1964.

Civil appeals against the decision of the Court of Appeal may be made to the Federal Court with the leave of the Federal Court. This jurisdiction is provided in the section 96(a) and 96(b) within the Courts of Judicature Act 1964.

Court   *of*   *Appeal*

Jurisdiction

As for the Court of Appeal, it hears the appeals from High Court in civil or criminal matters and it is the only court that has limited function as an appellate court. In other words, it did not hear the cases for the first time but review the cases from the lower courts instead. The Court of Appeal is also the highest court for cases decided by the High Court in its appellate or revisionary jurisdiction.

High   *Court*

Jurisdiction

the High Court can perform as a court of first instance when it can hear cases under its jurisdiction for the first time or appellate court when it hears appeals from the Sessions Court and Magistrates' Court. In addition, the High Court usually hears cases that are clearly outside the jurisdiction of the lower courts.

Why we need to have this three hierarchy of courts.

This three hierarchy of courts are important because the hierarchy provides structure and clarity to administration and dispensation of justice as different levels of courts are dealing with different levels and layers of disputes that can range from a simple to a complex matter. As the position of a court in the hierarchy determines the type of cases that it can deal with, this allows for specialization of each court to deal with those cases as the judges will be familiar and well versed to handle them in their capacities.

In addition, the decision of higher courts are binding on those of lower courts allows for simple yet effective functioning of the doctrine of the precedent. The doctrine of precedent allows for the application of the law to be decided with as much consistency and fairness as possible. Also, the court hierarchy is arranged in such a way that allows for smooth appeals process

(Department of Accounting, College of Administration and Economics/ University of Basra, Iraq)
hisham noori hussain AL-hashimy 978-1-62265-912-8 (online) 978-1-62265-913-5 (paper)

without the need for additional separate appellate courts for each original court as this will unnecessarily slow the process of administration of justice. When there is no satisfaction over the decision of a case, an appeal of that case can be made simply by applying to a higher court. The court hierarchy ensures that the parties who are concerned with the case know where the appeal will be considered because there is a clear direction in the appeal process within the court hierarchy.

Why we need to have the Court of Appeal?

The Court of Appeal is important for its sole function of being the only court with appellate jurisdiction instead of being the court of first instance or original jurisdiction. Being the court that is limited only to appellate jurisdiction means that the Court of Appeal does not hear cases for the first time but hears appeals from lower court specifically.

The Court of Appeal is also considered as the highest court for the cases decided by the High Court in its appellate or revisionary jurisdiction. In other words, the High Court cases that are originally from Subordinate courts such as Session Court and Magistrates' Court will end up on Court of Appeal instead of Federal Court and this means that the Court of Appeal have the final say on the cases from lower courts.

Why we need to but appeal court between Federal Court and High Court?

The appeal process from High Court to Federal Court is fundamentally important because it provides a clear direction or flow that allows the parties that are concerned with a particular suit to be able to appeal to a higher court in the hierarchy of courts when they are not satisfied with the decision of the court. Furthermore, there is consistency as the concerned parties will know where the case will end up and it will be just one horizontal direction from lower to higher courts instead of having a vertical direction when a case that is being appealed have to be transferred around specialist appellate courts in

(Department of Accounting, College of Administration and Economics/ University of Basra, Iraq)
hisham noori hussain AL-hashimy   978-1-62265-912-8 (online)   978-1-62265-913-5 (paper)

the same jurisdiction. In other words, there is a precise and exact flow of cases being appealed from lower courts to higher courts and the decision of higher courts bind those of lower courts by overruling them when the higher courts decided that they are not satisfied and disagreed with the way of judges   from   lower   courts   in   deciding   those   cases.

Explain the jurisdiction of court and why the Court of Appeal became second in the hierarchy.

The jurisdiction of courts is organized in such a way that the highest court in the land will be the Federal Court, followed by the Court of Appeal and High Court respectively. These courts are known as Superior courts and they generally bind those of lower courts or Subordinate courts such as Sessions Court   and   Magistrates'   Court. The Court of Appeal became second in the hierarchy because it is just below the Federal Court which is the highest or apex court in the court hierarchy. This also means that when a case is being appealed from High Court, it will end up first on Court of Appeal instead of Federal Court by virtue of court hierarchy.

Why Court of Appeal became the highest court and why we need the highest   court?

The Court of Appeal is said to be highest court for High Court cases that are originally from the Subordinate courts such as Sessions Court and Magistrates' Court and this reflects Court of Appeals' power in reviewing High Court's appellate and revisionary jurisdiction. The reason of requiring the Court of Appeal to be the highest court in having final say for those High Court cases from lower courts is so that Federal Court did not have to deal with these cases. Moreover, this arrangement means that the Federal Court would be more specialized and suited in dealing and handling cases that have more complicated and complex matters. Furthermore, this proves to be helpful as the Court of Appeal acts a filter to deal with often high volume of appeal cases while those cases that merit the attention of Federal Court

120

judges will be handled by them when the Federal Court grants leave to hear and decide them.

Why we need to have High Court before the Court of Appeal and the Federal Court?

Despite being the lowest in the hierarchy of Superior courts, the position of the High Court is very important because it is a court of first instance as well as an appellate court. The High Court is said to be a court of first instance or of original jurisdiction as it can hear cases under its jurisdiction for the first time. Furthermore, it also functions as an appellate court when it hears appeals from the lower courts such as Sessions Court and Magistrates' Court. It must also be noted that offences or claims that cannot be tried in the lower courts will be tried in the High Court instead.

What is the reason for existing these three courts?

The existence of the three courts is absolutely essential because it is the key to administration and dispensation of justice in this country. It is vital to have these courts because they are the building blocks of justice in upholding rule of law and its application in the spirit of the Federal Constitution. The arrangement of this court hierarchy allows for consistent application of well-established and proven binding precedents that stand against time. In other words, these good laws have been successfully applied in court decisions of cases time and time again. However, if a party have a stronger cause or claim to prove why their particular case should be distinguished from the established precedent or there is a stronger argument to change the said precedent, the court is flexible enough to decide in that party's favor. In fact, the decision by the higher courts will change the precedent and the lower courts are bound to follow it unless there is further development of case laws that can change the precedent when it is considered as obsolete.

Another reason behind the existence of the three courts is the hierarchy allows for different levels of specialization as the High Court usually absorbs and deals with bulk of the cases while the Court of Appeal will deal with cases that are appealed from the High Court, leaving the usually more complicated cases appealed from the Court of Appeal to be dealt by the Federal Court as the highest court in the land. In short, the nature of the cases being handled by each court will ensure each of them will be more familiar and experienced in dealing and deciding them in increased speed and clarity. This enables the courts to be decisive and efficient in determining the construction of law and its application in those cases. It highlights how the court hierarchy encourages the promotion of certainty and rule of law as well as upholding the Federal Constitution. Furthermore, the existence of the three courts provides structure for speedy dispensation of justice as each court is specialized to deal with cases that are in their scope of power as well as saving time and money that are otherwise wasteful in deciding the cases.

In Malaysia, there are **4 major business vehicles** that allowed under SSM (Suruhanjaya Syarikat Malaysia) Registration. They are sole proprietorship, general partnership, limited liability partnership (LLP) and company. Each of the business vehicles are having their own characteristics and governed by different governing legislation. Partnership and company are two business vehicles that accepted widely due to the fact that with bigger scale business entity and higher risk exposure, several people will tend to form a company or partnership together to reduce the capital contribution as well as risk. In this section, we will discuss the difference between partnership and company in details.

Nature of Organization

Partnership is a type of business organization that is owned by two or more individuals. It is a little harder and more expensive to organize than the proprietorship. The owners of the partnership are known as partners. For company, it is a type of business organization that is owned by shareholders and it is structured as a separate legal entity under the operation of law. The ownership of a corporation is divided into shares of stock. A corporation issues the stock to individuals or other businesses, who then become owners or stockholders, of the corporation.

Registration/Enforcement of legal right

General partnership as registered by agreement. The partnership has same entity as the partners and governs under Partnership Act 1961 (Act 135). Agreement will define the partners with right to operate the business. Partners have the right to share the management. Shareholders in a company are created by registration by statue. It is legally known as separate entity from the business and governs by The Company Act 1965 (Act 125). Memorandum defines the right of shareholders and operation team for the business. It could be different team of ownership and representative management in operation.

Liability

General partnership is having unlimited liability while company is having limited liability by shareholding of the shareholders. Unlimited liability indicates that under a circumstance a business fails or declared bankrupt creditors can sue the sole proprietor's owner for all debts owed to respective merchants. This means personal asset, personal income and employment income are all liable. Limited liability of shareholders' contribution to this company is limited to the amount specified on their unpaid shares. Under the condition of the company becomes insolvent or goes into liquidation, members are not obligated to pay off the company's debts if and unless any one of the members gives a personal guarantee.

Duration of existence

Partnership could be dissolved by court order, agreement of partners, death or bankruptcy of any partners. For company, as the company is different entity from owner, the death of shareholders does not dissolve the business. The company can only be dissolved via striking-off or winding up the business.

Transfer of interest

Partners in partnership does not have right to openly transfer the share or interest. For a public company, the share can be transfer freely in open market.

Formalities

General partnership does not involved much formalities as long has the entity maintain a basic financial report and account for taxation purposes. Company involves more formalities as they need auditors to verify and report financial affairs, reports, accounts and statement. For public company, they need to publish the financial report and activities to the shareholders. In addition, they must have company secretary for Annual General Meeting (AGM), board and shareholders meeting.

Limits of size

General partnership allows partner size of 2 to 20 partners. Under SSM rules, partnership for professional practice does not have maximum limit. In terms of company, private company allowed minimum 2 up to 50 shareholders in a private company (SD Bud), while public company (Bud) does not have limit in the number of shareholders.

Raising capital

General partnership could raise the initial capital from own saving and any other personal resources. Company could raise unlimited capital via go public by issuing share or contribution from the shareholders.

in Budget 2013, a new business entity called Limited Liability Partnership (LLP) was introduced. The LLP was introduced to address the unlimited liability exposure in partnerships. This enable the local businesses and entrepreneurs another option to run their operations in a more competitive manner with different management of risk. As compared to LLP, a conventional partnership could expose the partners to unlimited liability which is higher in risk exposure and legal entitlement. In this section, difference between partnership and limited liability partnership will be discussed in details.

Nature of Organization

Partnership, a conventional partnership is an association of any kind including joint venture, syndicates between parties who agree to combine their rights, power, and skill, for the purpose of carrying on business and share the profit. Limited liability partnership is a business structure that combines the feature of incorporated company and a partnership in terms of liability, dissolution of business, legal capacity, entity and others.

Registration/Enforcement of legal right

General partnership as registered by agreement. The partnership has same entity as the partners and governs under Partnership Act 1961 (Act 135). Agreement will define the partners with right to operate the business. Partners have the right to share the management. For LLP, it is regulated by Limited Liability Partnership Act 2012 (Act 743) where the name of LLP must have "LLP" nomenclature. A LLP is a legal person at law where it possesses a separate legal personality from the partners. It can sue and be sued in its own legal capacity.

Liability

General partnership is having unlimited liability while company is having limited liability by shareholding of the shareholders. Unlimited liability indicates that under a circumstance a business fails or declared bankrupt creditors can sue the sole proprietor's owner for all debts owed to respective merchants. This means personal asset, personal income and employment income are all liable. In a limited liability partnership, the partner is not personally liable for an obligation of the LLP by reason of being a partner in the business. LLP has characteristic of a company which is limited liability. However, if partners involved wrongful act in the course of business, he is still exposed to liabilities to a third party.

Duration of existence

Partnership could be dissolved by court order, agreement of partners, death or bankruptcy of any partners. For LLP, it could be dissolved by Court order, LLP has ceased to operate and discharged all debts and liabilities, the LLP is not in operation or contravened with LLP Act.

Transfer of interest

Partners in partnership does not have right to openly transfer the share or interest and applies the same to limited liability partnership.

Formalities

General partnership does not involved much formalities as long has the entity maintain a basic financial report and account for taxation purposes. For LLP, it also does not have statutory requirement for account to be audited. But it should keep sufficient accounting and records to enable explanation of financial position and tax purpose. A special feature for LLP is the business need to appoint a Compliance Officer from partners. Compliance officer will responsible for compliance requirement such as registration of particulars regarding the LLP, maintaining documentation, accounting record of the LLP business and be the chargeable person for income tax purpose on filling of tax return, payment of tax, and any other tax related matters.

Limits of size

General partnership allows partner size of 2 to 20 partners. Under SSM rules, partnership for professional practice does not have maximum limit. In terms of LLP, the size of business is ranged from minimum 2 to unlimited as maximum partners.

Raising capital

General partnership could raise the initial capital from own saving and any other personal resources. LLP also raise initial capital from partners and known as partner contribution. This is similar for both conventional and LLP partnerships. However, only paid up amounts are recognized as capital contribution in LLP and LLP agreement must document the amount and method of capital contribution of partners.

(Department of Accounting, College of Administration and Economics/ University of Basra, Iraq)
hisham noori hussain AL-hashimy   978-1-62265-912-8 (online) 978-1-62265-913-5 (paper)

127

CHAPTER 4

Creative Accounting and Ethical commitment

The Relationship between Ethical Commitment and Creative Accounting Practices

1.1 Background of the Research

The subject of creative accounting has received importance due to the recent serious accounting scandals that occurred in large companies. The collapse of the large companies in the world such as Enron and WorldCom along with Arthur Anderson which was considered one of the biggest companies in accounting as a result of involving in unethical practices in preparing the financial statements (Toffler & Rheingold, 2004). This has led the United States of America (USA) to enforce the law of Sarbanes-Oxley Act. Many studies have been conducted in identifying the motives for these companies to act in unethical ways (Chef Fins, 2013).

Creative accounting is defined "a process of manipulating accounting to take advantages of the loopholes in accounting rules and the choices of measurement and disclosure practices" (Nasser, 1993). Another definition is given by Gowthorpe and Amati (2005) as "the deliberate distortion of the communication between entities and shareholders by the activities of financial statement preparers who wish to change the content of the message being transmitted". Thus, creative accounting does not violate the law or the standards of accounting. It is mainly based on finding loopholes in accounting rules that enable the professional accountant to alter the financial income of companies.

(Department of Accounting, College of Administration and Economics/ University of Basra, Iraq)
hisham noori hussain AL-hashimy   978-1-62265-912-8 (online) 978-1-62265-913-5 (paper)

Professional accountants are the main responsible for reporting the financial situation of companies. The ethical commitments of the professional accountants are important in the workplace, especially when they are preparing the financial statements. The professional accountants must apply these ethical commitments, to serve the interest groups of the financial information users. However, the users of financial statements are taking the decision based on the information that is provided by the team of the professional accountants, and there are some cases of the creative accounting practices from Worldwide and Malaysia, had affected the decisions of those who are using the financial information. However, the Code of Ethics for Professional Accountants (IFAC) has listed the components of ethical commitment for professional accountants to include (1) integrity, (2) objectivity, (3) professional competence and due care, (4) confidentiality, and last (5) professional behavior (IFAC, 2006). These five components are investigated and compared in this study. Other codes of ethics were mainly based on the principle of the IFAC and did a reproduction of these codes of ethics such as Certified public accountant (CPA). Minor changes of the code of ethics can be found in the code of ethics of National Board of Accountants and Auditors (NBAA). The new principles in NBAA include tax practice and cross boarder activities.

In Malaysia, the practices of creative accounting that had been done from the period of 2007 to 2011 in some large public listed companies such as Tran smile Group Bud, and Megan Media Bud has increased the interest in the field of creative accounting in Malaysia (Norman et al. 2011). Most of the countries have issued ethical code of conduct to urge professional accountant to adhere to these code and produce, reliable, true, and fair annual reports of companies. However, the degree of adhering to these codes is varied based on individual, organizational, cultural, and traditions perceptive. Thus, the need arise to find the degree to which Malaysian accountant are adhering to the code of ethics and to find to what extent these ethics can prevent the conduct of creative accounting practices. Therefore, this study is meant to investigate these relationships and produce practical recommendation for decision makers to improve the environment under which the professional accountants work. In this study, the relationships among each component of the ethical commitments and creative accounting practices are investigated.

1.2 Problem of the Research

Creative accounting has a major influence on the financial situation of the companies. Producing misleading reports that mislead the decision of stakeholders can lead to bad decision making of stakeholders (Shah et al. 2011). Professional accountant are responsible for preparing the financial reports. The user of financial information, expect professional accountants to be highly competent, reliable, and objective (Henderson et al. 2013). However, the professional accountants should not only be fully qualified but must also possess a high degree of professional integrity (Burks, 2006). Thus, the ethics of accountants are highly significant because of the main function of accountants is to provide helpful information to users (Raman, 2003).

The creative accounting is the manipulation of financial statements. Therefore, it seems that the purpose of creative accounting is to mask the entity's true financial position and performance. By creative accounting can hide the important information from the users of financial statements (Elias, 2004). Thus, researcher highlighted the role of ethics as a cure for the creative accounting practices (Al Momamani, 2013).

The great majority of the studies conducted on the problem of creative accounting concerns large countries with developed capital markets (Bara lexis, 2004). Furthermore, regulators of accounting profession in Malaysia are very strict on the issue of creative accounting. Many cases of creative accounting practices have recorded in Malaysia. These cases include some public listed companies such as Infix Technologies Holdings Berthed, Granaries Corporation Berthed, Cosmo Technology Industrial Berthed, Memes Technology Berthed, GP Ocean Food Berthed, Polymath Holdings Berthed, Tran smile Group Berthed, Megan Media Holdings Berthed

Velayutham (2003) doubted the extent to which the code of ethics can create moral responsibility. He stated that the code only focuses on quality of the service provided by accountants rather than ethics. Thus, the principles of the code need to be examined. Rabin (2005) supported the belief that the effectiveness of the Code of Professional Conduct in constraining creative accounting needs to be examined. The problem of the study is that the lack of ethical commitments by some practitioners of the accounting profession leads to the creative accounting practices (Armstrong, Katz & Owen, 2003; Rabin, 2005; Osazevbaru, 2012; Bearish and Shale, 2014). However, ethical commitment is likely to prevent professional accountant from conducting creative accounting practices (Osazevbaru, 2012). Therefore, there is a question must be answered regarding the relationship between the creative accounting practice and the ethical commitment elements namely; (1) integrity, (2) objectivity, (3) professional competence and due care, (4) confidentiality, and (5) professional behavior, and to what extend element of ethical commitment could prevent the accounting from providing misleading information to the stakeholders.

1.3 Research Objectives

To identify the relationship between integrity and creative accounting practices.

To identify the relationship between objectivity and creative accounting practices.

To identify the relationship between professional competence and due care and creative accounting practices.

(Department of Accounting, College of Administration and Economics/ University of Basra, Iraq)
hisham noori hussain AL-hashimy   978-1-62265-912-8 (online) 978-1-62265-913-5 (paper)

To identify the relationship between confidentiality and creative accounting practices.

To identify the relationship between professional behavior and creative accounting practices.

1.4 Research Questions

The research questions of this study are:

1) Is there a relationship between integrity and creative accounting practices?

2) Is there a relationship between objectivity and creative accounting practices?

3) Is there a relationship between professional competence and due care and creative accounting practices?

4) Is there a relationship between confidentiality and creative accounting practices?

5) Is there a relationship between professional behavior and creative accounting practices?

1.5 The Significance of the Study

The study is important due to the lack of studies in the area of creative accounting practices in Malaysia. Therefore, the study will add to the database of creative accounting practices and ethical commitment. In addition, the study will increase the awareness toward the creative accounting practices and the role of ethical commitments in healing this phenomenon. The study will provide the decision makers and the educational institution with the factors that heal the professional accounting practices so that they can focuses to implant these values on the next generation of accountant.

1.6 Scope of the Research

This study focuses on the ethical commitment elements that are listed by IFAC (2006). These elements include (1) integrity, (2) objectivity, (3) professional competence and due care, (4) confidentiality, and last (5) professional behavior. The IFAC chosen because most other code was built based on the IFAC code of ethics. The study is limited to the relationship between ethical commitments' elements and the creative accounting practices in Malaysia from the perspective of professional accountants at Malaysian institutions.

1.7 Summary

This chapter has presented the background of the study. Ethical commitment of the professional accountant can be a cure for the creative accounting practices. Few studies have investigated these issues. This study is investigating the impact of the ethical commitment elements on the creative accounting practices. The chapter presented the research objectives and questions along with the research significance and scope.

(Department of Accounting, College of Administration and Economics/ University of Basra, Iraq)
hisham noori hussain AL-hashimy   978-1-62265-912-8 (online) 978-1-62265-913-5 (paper)

LITERATURE REVIEW

2.0 Introduction

This chapter discusses the importance of the ethical commitment and its relationship with creative accounting practices. The chapter starts by introducing the topic of creative accounting, definitions, techniques, reasons behind creative accounting and the prevention of creative accounting. Second section presents the definition of ethical commitment and the codes of ethical commitment along with the elements of the ethical commitment. Lastly, the chapter presents the theoretical framework of the study along with the related hypotheses.

2.1 Creative Accounting

Many names can be associated with creative accounting. In United State (US) the term is known as creative accounting or earning management. While in Europe, the term is known as creative accounting. Some other countries call the creative accounting as incoming smoothing, earnings smoothing, and cosmetic accounting, and financial engineering. In this section, the definition of creative accounting is discussed along with the practices and techniques, reasons behind the creative accounting practices, and prevention of creative accounting. According to Colace, creative accounting is defined as a cumulus of accounting information practices, at the limit of legitimacy, practiced by some economic entities in order to beautify the image of the financial position and the economic-financial performances (Colace as cited by Baldacci, Began & Valdo, 2009).

2.1.1 Definition of Creative Accounting

Creative accounting is defined as "a process of manipulating accounting to take advantages of the loopholes in accounting rules and the choices of measurement and disclosure practices" (Nasser, 1993). According to Amati, Blake, and Dowd's (1999), creative accounting is a process which the accountants use their knowledge of the provisions and accounting rules to manipulate the financial statements. Moreover, creative accounting was defined by Gowthorpe and Amati (2005) as "the deliberate distortion of the communication between entities and shareholders by the activities of financial statement preparers who wish to change the content of the message being transmitted". It was described as one of the practices that some companies use to gain benefits in short or long term (Maria and Pavlov, 2013).

Based on above, the definition highlights the use of creative accounting to provide misleading information about the financial statement or income statement of a particular company. The definition of Nasser (1993) is adopted in this study because it serves the purpose of this study.

2.1.2 Creative Accounting Areas and Techniques

Previous studies in creative accounting have identified many areas and techniques of creative accounting. In a study conducted by Amati and Gowthorpe (2010) to identify the creative accounting and its nature along with incidence and ethical issues, they pointed out that the creative accounting techniques that might occur include issues such as regulatory flexibility, dearth of regulation, management interest, time of conducting some big transactions, presenting encouraging financial statement. Similarly, the study of Salome et al., (2012) indicates that the creative accounting techniques are regulatory flexibility, and dearth of regulation.

(Department of Accounting, College of Administration and Economics/ University of Basra, Iraq)
hisham noori hussain AL-hashimy   978-1-62265-912-8 (online) 978-1-62265-913-5 (paper)

Shah, Butt and Tariq (2011) investigate the use and the abuse of creative accounting techniques and pointed out that there are some techniques that are useful to be used while other considered misleading. Akimbo and Ibanichuka (2012) investigated the creative accounting practices in Nigerian banks. The findings indicated that the major reason for creative accounting practices in Nigerian banks is to boost the market value of shares; users of accounting information are adversely affected by the practice of creative accounting; accounting principles and rules should be streamlined to reduce diversities of professional judgment in financial reporting. They have mentioned that there are many techniques that are being used. This includes unavoidable degree of estimation, judgment, and prediction, artificial transaction, and genuine transactions.

Moldovan, Ache, and Aram, (2010) studied the role of creative accounting as a technique of accounts manipulation in contrast with the fair view presentation, and the ethics of accounting profession. In this study, the authors reviewed the opinions of different authors on the subject while contrasting both fraud and professional ethics with creative accounting. In addition, they explained the inverse causal relationship between creative accounting and fair view principle. The study reviewed the writings of other authors regarding creative account in order to find or recommend some solutions to this problem, which threaten the fair presentation. The recommended solutions in this area are related to accounting rules and professional accounting ethics. These solutions are characterized with its practicability and can be put in practice by the company itself and by other interested users.

Regarding the areas of creative accounting, the study of Sansui et al., (2012) provide a description of the areas that give the opportunities for creative accounting to be applied. These include financial statements, namely revenue, and assets and amortization policies. Other study by Yama (2013) has given some other areas where creative accounting can be applied. These

136

include tangible assets, goodwill, depreciation, and inventories, provisions for liabilities and charges, and construction contracts. Similarly, the study of Agawam (2008) has identified many other areas that include off- balance sheet financing, inventory system, modifying depreciation policy, leasing, increase income, manipulating expenses, acquiring goodwill. Shah and Butt (2011) pointed out that the creative accounting practices can occur in the areas of accounting policies, changes in accounting policy, overvalue closing stock, provisions for bad debts, legal obligations, and the current profits. In addition, book false gains through sales purchase back, playing with debits and credits, big bath charges, creative acquisition accounting, cookie jar reserves, materiality, revenue recognition are the areas for financial manipulation.

Li (2006) reviewed that the income management manipulation of expenses: (deferring costs, reserve accounting, capitalization of expenses), overvaluing assets, concealment of, losses or liabilities, tampering taxation, off balance-sheet financing, inventory: (year-end manipulations, Net Realizable Value (NRV), overheads), extraordinary and exceptional items, acquisition goodwill, leasing transactions, capitalization of research and development, expenditure, depreciation policy changing are the way for creative accounting. Raman et al., (2013) analyzed, the techniques that are used for accounting manipulation which are cookie jar reserve, big bath, big bet on the future, " flushing" the investment portfolio, "throw out" a problem child, introducing new standard, write off of long term operating assets, sale/leaseback, operating versus non-operating income, early retirement of debt use of derivatives, shrink the ship.

2.1.3 Reasons behind Creative Accounting

Creative accounting has taken the attention of researchers and practitioners due to the interest of companies to project better financial pictures of their operations (Li, 2006). The creative accounting practices can influence the

137

market share and the prices of the share of the company along with the value of the company and this is only possible when investors do not know that there is creative accounting practices took place (Osazevbaru and Salon, 2012).

Creative accounting practices still exist and they will not stop as long as the companies want to use them for their purposes and interest (Shah and Butt, 2011). Boost share price in the stock market are the main reason for creative accounting practices as noticed by Cletus and Ibanichuka (2012). Another reason was identified by Kama et al., (2012) is to avoid paying tax as creative accounting can enlarge the expense and reduce the amount of taxes that the company has to pay to the government. This is because the taxes are calculated based on the net income of the company. Thus, companies would try to minimize their income to reduce the amount of money that they have to pay as tax of income. For Ibanichuka and Ihendinihu (2012) the creative accounting practices were increased due to many reasons that include the payment of dividends, the choice of accounting method, the Category of 'extraordinary item' in the Profit and Loss Account, the Quality of Earnings report of the Income Statement by External Auditors, the Ethical of Accountants, and lastly the Weaknesses of the Control System.

Agawam (2008) listed many reasons for companies to be involved in the creative accounting practices. These include the debt structure of the companies, the financial distress, and the increasingly the competitive environment, practices of internal control mechanism, the ownership structure of the company, and the interest of the Chief executive officers (CEO) to increase the profits figures thus his payments and rewards will increase accordingly. Vera (2010) compared between the developed and developing countries in term of the creative accounting practices. The findings showed that in developed countries, creative accounting is more prevalent. Gherkin and Baldacci (2011) related the entire financial crisis that took place to the practices of creative accounting. They gave examples of companies that have used the creative accounting practices to beautify their income statement and encourage investors to buy the companies' share. They called for considering all the parties that involved in creative accounting to be held responsible for this kind of crime. They added that the creative accounting practices would not end until the reasons that encourage companies to do these practices end.

Deferens et al., (2013) pointed out that the creative accounting practices might more frequently occur in an environment that are categorized as rapidly changing environment. Yama (2013) related the creative accounting practices to the loopholes that are existed in the accounting standards and regulations. As a cure to the creative accounting practices, they called for involving the corporate governance that can observe the activities of the company and the managers using independents directors who are elected by the shareholders. According to Shah et al., (2011) currently, the creative accounting practices are difficult to be controlled due to the variety of the standards and regulation and the increase of the interaction in the business world. They identified many reason behind the use of creative accounting. These include, meeting the organizational targets and goals, meeting the external expectation of the company performance, providing income smoothing, window dressing for initial public offering or a loan, for tax reduction purposes, and changes in the management structures.

The creative accounting practices can affect the company reputation as well as operations and income. A study conducted in Taiwan by Chen (2007) found that those companies who have been involved in creative accounting reported low income after tax compare with those who have clean records. Abiding et al., (2012) revealed that the practice of creative accounting in whatever form is an attempt to gain advantage of a form. According to Raman et al., (2013) the motivation of creative accounting which are as the following: 'stock market incentives, signaling or concealing private information, political costs, personal interest, internal motives, management compensation contract motivations, lending contracts motivations and regulatory motivations'.

Based on above, there are many reasons for a company to be involved in creative accounting practices. These reasons are mainly related to the company financial situation and the desire to hide critical financial fact about the company. Mainly, the reason behind the creative accounting for public listed companies is to increase the price of share and to reduce the amount of tax that they have to pay. For private and public companies, the aims are also to increase the value of the company and enhance its ability to ask for loan from banks. These reasons are mainly taking place in Malaysia as well as in other countries. However, the practices of creative accounting are higher in the developed countries compared with the developing countries.

2.1.4 Prevention of Creative Accounting

Creative accounting has become a challenge for financial bodies and government that are trying to protect the investors. Many laws around the world have been enacted to discourage the creative accounting practices. Large restriction on creative accounting could be seen at so-called harmonization of financial reporting and by application of mandatory IFRS (International Financial Reporting Standards) IAS, which are international guidelines for accounting and also preparation and presentation of financial statements published by the International Accounting Standards Board (IASB International Accounting Standards Board). IFRS would have "forced" most of the companies follow practices that are authentic and comparable. The changes would apply to understanding the concepts of assets, liabilities, costs, revenues, capital (Fiserv, 2005)

However, many research related the prevention of creative accounting to establishment of ethical commitment and to the ethical behavior of the professional accountant who are in charge of preparing the financial statement and the income statement (Al Mopani and Obeisant, 2013). Hotshot (2013) determine the creative accounting can be detection by internal audit, and the internal audit adds values to control and monitoring environment within business units such as buying points and depots to detect fraud. Ghost (2010) suggested that to minimize and prevention the creative accounting practice and fraudulent is to take action by the responsible bodies and agencies efficient of audit, strong regulation, modify company act, reduction of the choices of accounting treatment in accounting standards, and improvement the quality of corporate governance. Abiding et al., (2012) explored the best way to prevent the creative accounting in real work is to apply preventive measures, since the general accepted accounting principle create a gap that authorize the practices of creative accounting.

Al Mopani and Obeisant (2013) investigate that the auditors' independency, integrity, and objectivity affects in practice auditors' ability to detect the practices of creative accounting. However, the auditors' ability to detect the practices of the creative accounting is affected by the entire group of audit ethics more than their independency, integrity, and objectivity. Raman et al., (2013) identify that 'the rigorous accounting standard, awareness of audit committee, corporate governance and consciousness and the morality of the stake holders play a vital role to control earnings management'.

Overall, it can be seen that despite the strict laws and the punishment that those companies receive when they practice creative accounting, the creative accounting practice have not finished yet. The need for ethical and self-commitment is more important that laws and punishment. Ethically committed professional accountant can be the most effective cure for the creative accounting practices. The international code of professional accounting ethics stated that there are five main elements of ethical commitment. These are the integrity, objectivity, professional competence and due care, confidentiality, and professional behavior. Accountant must adhere to these principles so that the influence of creative accounting practices can reduced or ended. However, it is not clear which of these values are the most important one. Thus, the present study is trying to identify the influence of element of ethical commitment on the creative accounting practices.

2.2 Ethical Commitments

Ethical commitment is defined as the extent to which the individual adheres to ideal moral values and their regulatory enforcement within her/his professional community (Dendron, Sunday & Lam, 2006). Accounting profession and accountants as the performers of this profession are significant elements of the social order. Awareness of the accountants about the ethical problems of their profession and their resistance to the non-ethical demands and pressures increase their respect for their profession and affect their professional commitment positively. The level of professional commitment of an accountant who behaves in unethical way as the result of either administrative or personal choice is different from that of an accountant who behaves in ethical way (Umar & Dozer, 2011).

Bailey (1995) suggests that professional ethics and values are the product of a ''golden age'' of professionalism that has since passed, and that key ethical standards have not been successfully translated on the workplace to the younger generation. Simply stated, these critics suggest that changes in the context of professional work have made the accounting profession more susceptible to logic of commercial gain than professional independence and objectivity.

In this section, the definition of ethics along with the meaning and overview of ethical commitment is discussed.

2.2.1 Definition of Ethic

Ethics is something that human gain from their culture, values, norms, religions, and parents. Fleet (1991) define ethics as "standards or morals a person sets for himself or herself regarding what is good and or right and wrong". In addition, Napa (2010) pointed out that ethical behavior as a good or expected type of conduct, which is a desired moral type of behavior or legal behavior from a professional. Unethical behavior can simply mean unacceptable behavior. The behavior devoid of good, it is bad act or an illegal act punishable by law. There is absolutely no room for unethical behavior in the professional world. Thus, ethical commitment is something bigger than following the rule and regulation of the accounting bodies. It is about being ethical, honest, and trustworthy. Ethical commitment is likely to prevent professional accountant from conducting creative accounting practices (Osazevbaru, 2012)

2.2.2 Ethical Commitments or Code of Ethics

Professional accountants add more credibility to financial information and financial statements. They can play an active role in reducing the effects of this problem. These professional accountants are qualified to detect these practices of creative accounting because they are supposed to have good knowledge regarding accounting and auditing professions. The questionable issue is not about the competence of accountant, but about their ethics. Some interested people believe that professional accountant' ethics are more important than their competence. They believe that when auditors follow the ethical rules of their profession, they will be able to play more important role in detecting the different methods of creative accounting practices, and they will be able to add enough solutions to this negative practice. Many calls have been made for an environment that guides practitioner to adhere ethics through three elements represented by the existence of clear guidelines for ethics, reward committed to these guidelines, and to punish the offending it,

(Department of Accounting, College of Administration and Economics/ University of Basra, Iraq)
hisham noori hussain AL-hashimy   978-1-62265-912-8 (online) 978-1-62265-913-5 (paper)

and whenever there is a defect or deficiency in one of these elements whenever upset the balance of commitment to ethics (Airway, 2007).

Users of accounting information require more credible data to take good investment and credit decisions. Creative accounting practices reduce the expected benefits of financial information, and may convert this information from useful to non-useful information for the purposes of users' decisions. Therefore, these users may take ineffective and inefficient decisions because they depended on manipulated accounting information.

As a result, users will be unable to achieve their investment, credit, and other objectives. Auditors provide users of financial statements with more trust, faith, and credibility, because they have the right to depend on credible information and to be sure that the financial statements had been prepared based on the Generally Accepted Accounting Principles (GAAP), and these statements represent the actual events occurred during the accounting period (Al Momamani, 2013).

An ethical code of conduct is very important because stakeholders expect professional accountants to comply with it (Delaney, 2005). Ziegenfuss and Singhapakdi (1994) found that the ethical code of conduct influences professional accountants because they believe it guides their work. The ethical code of conduct is also said to have more effect on professional accountants than personal moral philosophies (Delaney, 2005). Professional accountants, like other professionals, need to comply with the ethical code of conduct because non-compliance results in penalties (England, 1998).

Thus, the ethical code of conduct is an effective tool that can increase public trust in the financial reports prepared by professional accountants (England, 1998). Whilst the main objective of the ethical code of conduct is to uphold the integrity of accounting profession, it benefits stakeholders as well.

Well known ethical code of conduct such as the International Financial Reporting Standards (IFRS) with USA Generally Accepted Accounting Principles (GAAP) must be followed to avoid the creative accounting practices. Ethics must be merged with the business conduct so that they can have an impact on the creative accounting practices (Mitchel, 2009).

Hormone and Pasco (2012) pointed out that the lack of moral and ethical principles in accounting would make preconditions to realize some "legal fraud," not essentially associated with creativity, however rather to the weakness of an accounting system while not rules and moral principles, reducing the quality of financial information. In addition, the accounting professionals, particularly auditors and financial consultants, have the ethical duty not solely to adopt associate moral behavior, however additionally to insure that those they advise are conscious of their own moral responsibilities.

The professionals accounting have to practice the accounting ethics, and they need specific education to apply that, for the professionals accounting to achieve that level of morals, they should know the effect of right and bad actions of ethical behavior. Besides that, there are the rules they also must to follow but only the rules itself not enough in the work environment, it must combine with the values of the persons that they are carrying to come out with good decision and right judgment (Unsurely et al., 2010).

Clayton, Staten and Lynch (2010) pointed out that the social pressure has an effect on professional accounting ethical reasoning. Furthermore, for those who with conformity, pressure will result in a low ethical decision.

Black et al., (2010) pointed out the role of ethics training and its influence on moral motivation, reasoning, and ethical intention. They found that the influence of ethics training is dependent on age, gender, culture, and demographics of the accountant.

Fisher and McCormack (2009) pointed out that sensitively of ethical commitments of professionals accounting has increased. This is because of the public interest in the financial reports. However, there is no important amendment seen for integrity. Umar and Dozer (2011) linked the professional behavior to the ethical decision-making. Ogbonna and Ebimobowei (2012) linked the quality of financial reports to the ethical accounting standards. Taco (2010) related the ethical problem to the management's expectations opposed to the principles of professional ethics; the desire to be promoted; the desire to earn money quickly; personal obligations or obligations of companions.

Koumbiadis and Opera (2008) pointed out that the perception of the ethical behavior has become more important. This has resulted in producing many ethical code of conduct. Coho (1992) refers to the importance of the in creating ethical commitment and guiding, resolving ethical issues, and enhancing the professional accountant image along with the increase of public confidence in professional, and make the ethical aspect at work more sentient. Similarly, Pflugrath, Bennie and Chen (2007) refer to the importance of code of ethics and link it to the positive impact of the performance and judgment of professional accountant. For Jamshidinavid and Kamahi (2012) the involvement in ethical practice is dependent on the willingness of individual. They stated "An individual's willingness and motivation has been recognized as a crucial factor in engaging in ethical decision making."

Professional accountant are encourage adhering to the Code of Ethics for Professional Accountants that was issued and update periodically by the International Ethics Standards Board for Accountants (IESBA) which specifies five elements that must be adhered to by professional accountant. These are (1) integrity; (2) objectivity; (3) professional competence and due care; (4) confidently; and (5) professional behavior. The present study is investigating the impact of these five elements on the creative accounting practices in Malaysia.

2.3 Elements of Ethical Commitment

Velayutham (2003) explains that professions need a code of ethics to reassure the public and clients of their members' responsibilities and thereby maintain members' integrity and reputations. The Code identifies the objectives of the accountancy profession as working to the highest standards of professionalism, attaining the highest levels of performance and meeting its responsibility to the public. To achieve these objectives, members have to observe a number of fundamental principles: integrity, objectivity, professional competence and due care, confidentiality, and professional behavior. Velayutham (2003) challenges the ability of the Code to establish the moral responsibility of the profession. He contends that the Code focuses primarily on the quality of the service provided by accountants and auditors and not on ethics. Thus the principle of the code needs to be examined.

The IFAC's membership includes 155 professional accounting bodies in 118 countries, representing more than 2.5 million accountants. A substantial number of professional accounting bodies in the world, including the ICAEW, have adopted the IFAC Code of Ethics in their own codes to meet their membership obligations to IFAC. The IESBA predicted that these codes of ethics must be followed to avoid the creative accounting practices. It is anticipated that also if the code are followed and applied properly, the creative accounting practices will be reduces. In the following subsection, the codes are deliberated.

2.3.1 Integrity

Smith (2003) responded to the Sarbanes-Oxley Act by suggesting that government rules and regulations cannot preserve a profession where people lack integrity. He suggests that leaders in the profession and academic "call individuals to excellence" and "inculcate in practitioners ethical behavior and personal integrity". According to the IFAC (2013) a professional accountant should be straightforward and honest in all professional and business relationships. Oxford Dictionary defines integrity as the quality of being honest and having strong moral principles. Integrity is the first principle in the ethical commitment. The IESBA pointed out that "a professional accounting must be straightforward and honest in all professional and business relationships" (IESBA, 2013). This include being straightforward and honest with all relationships. It is also being fair and trustworthy. The consistency in the face of adversity and in word and action are the characteristic of integrity (Polanski & Yammering, 2007). Peterson & Seligman, (2004) described those who act with authenticity and honesty by speaking and presenting the truth, presenting themselves in a genuine way with sincerity, showing no pretense, and taking responsibility for their own feelings and actions as having integrity. An accountant should uphold high ethical standards and maintain integrity in all their professional confidence, by stopping the fraudulent practices of creative accounting (Yeoman & Around, 2009). Integrity must serve as the organizing principle for accounting professional. Developing one's moral, ethical dimension is a central element in conducting accounting (Carroll, 1998)

In this study, professional accountant who has high level of integrity is expected to behave ethically and contributes to the decrease of the creative accounting practices in the organizations. Thus, the study proposes that integrity influence negatively the creative accounting practice i.e. integrity will reduce the creative accounting practice.

2.3.2 Objectivity

According to IFAC (2013), a professional accountant should not allow bias, conflict of interest or undue influence of others to override professional or business judgments. Business dictionary defines objectivity in accounting field as "accountant's reliance on verifiable evidence (such as delivery notes, invoices, orders, physical counts, paper or electronic trail) in the measurement of financial results. Objectivity is the view of accountants as objective appraisers of reality, .representing reality "as is" (Morgan, 1988). Objectivity makes it possible to compare financial statements of different firms with an assurance of reliability and uniformity".

According to the Chartered Institute of Management Accountants (CIMA), the principle of objectivity imposes an obligation on all professional accountants not to compromise their professional or business judgment because of bias, conflict of interest, or the undue influence of others. A professional accountant may be exposed to situations that may impair objectivity. It is impracticable to define and prescribe all such situations. A professional accountant shall not perform a professional service if a circumstance or relationship biases or unduly influences the accountant's professional judgment with respect to that service (CIMA, 2015).

For the purpose of achieving objectivity in accounting, a trust, fair and correct accounts should be prepared and fair and correct financial statement (Debacle, 2003). In the present study, professional accountant objectivity is expected to have a negative influence on creative accounting practices. The objectivity will reduce the creative accounting practices by professional accountant in Malaysia.

2.3.3 Professional Competence and Due Care

According to IFAC (2013), professional accountants have a continuing duty to maintain professional knowledge and skill at the level required to ensure that a client or employer receives competent professional service based on current developments in practice, legislation, and techniques. Professional accountants should act diligently and in accordance with applicable technical and professional standards when providing professional services (CIMA, 2015; IFAC, 2013)

Professional accountant are required to carry out their work with a proper regard for relevant technical and professional standards. This means that no one should undertake professional work, which they are not competent to perform. Competent professional service requires the exercise of sound judgment in applying professional knowledge and skill in the performance of such service. Professional competence may be divided into two separate phases: (a) Attainment of professional competence; and (b) Maintenance of professional competence.

The maintenance of professional competence requires a continuing awareness and an understanding of relevant technical, professional, and business developments. Continuing professional development enables a professional accountant to develop and maintain the capabilities to perform competently within the professional environment (IFAC, 2013).

Diligence encompasses the responsibility to act in accordance with the requirements of an assignment, carefully, thoroughly and on a timely basis. A professional accountant shall take reasonable steps to ensure that those working under the professional accountant's authority in a professional capacity have appropriate training and supervision. Where appropriate, a professional accountant shall make clients, employers or other users of the accountant's professional services aware of the limitations inherent in the services (IFAC, 2013).

Based on above, the present study predict that professional competence and due care could influence negatively the creative accounting practices. This is because a professional accountant who is competent and take care of his or her work would reduce the possibility for conducting creative accounting practices.

2.3.4 Confidentiality

According to IFAC (2013), a professional accountant should respect the confidentiality of information acquired as a result of professional and business relationships and should not disclose any such information to third parties without proper and specific authority unless there is a legal or professional right or duty to disclose. Confidential information acquired as a result of professional and business relationships should not be used for the personal advantage of the professional accountant or third parties.

According to CIMA (2015), the principle of confidentiality imposes an obligation on all professional accountants to refrain from disclosing or using confidential information. A professional accountant shall maintain confidentiality, including in a social environment, being alert to the possibility of inadvertent disclosure. He or she must maintain information disclosed by prospective client or employer within the firm. The professional accountant needs to comply with the principle of confidentiality continues even after the end of relationships between him or her and a client or employer. When a professional accountant changes employment or acquires a new client, the professional accountant is entitled to use prior experience. The professional accountant shall not, however, use or disclose any confidential information either acquired or received because of a professional or business relationship.

The book "Accountants' Roles and Responsibilities in Estates and Trusts" notes that, in most circumstances, the law considers the relationship between an accountant and client to be a confidential one. Confidential information is privileged information that generally is not known that a client shares with an accountant for a specific purpose. The accountant is obligated to protect this information from unauthorized disclosure or public release. Because accountants comply with the confidentiality principle, clients feel free to speak frankly and reveal relevant facts regarding accounting issues, enabling the accountant to act in the client's best interest (Glassman and Ciociola, 2009).

Based on above, professional accountant must not disclose information that is related to their employers. In this study, it is expected that the confidentiality will affect negatively the creative accounting practices in Malaysia.

2.3.5 Professional Behavior

According to IFAC (2013), a professional accountant should comply with relevant laws and regulations and should avoid any action that discredits the profession. The principle of professional behavior imposes an obligation on all professional accountants to comply with relevant laws and regulations and avoid any action that the professional accountant knows or should know may discredit the profession. This includes actions that a reasonable and informed third party, weighing all the facts and circumstances available to the professional accountant at that time, would be likely to conclude adversely affects the good reputation of the profession (CIMA, 2015).

As a minimum, the professional must comply with relevant laws and regulations. This means, for example, an accountant must abide by the laws that affect business and accounting, plus other regulations and standards that apply to that accountant and their work. These might be rules in the firm or workplace, or industry or professional rules. If there are rules to be followed, it is professional behavior to follow them, and unprofessional behavior to ignore or break them. Showing respect for the rules in this way enhances the individual's and the profession's reputation.

Based on above, it is expected that if the professional accountant adhere to the rules of professional behavior, they will reduce the likelihood of creative accounting practices in Malaysia. Thus, it is expected that professional behavior would affect negatively the creative accounting practices in Malaysia.

2.4 Theoretical Framework

The literature has focused on studies and reports regarding the ethical commitment and the creative accounting practices. Based on the review, ethical commitments consist of five elements which are (1) integrity, (2) objectivity, (3) professional competence and due care, (4) confidentiality, and (5) professional behavior (IFAC, 2006; 2013). Thus, the theoretical framework of this study is proposed as in Figure 2.1.

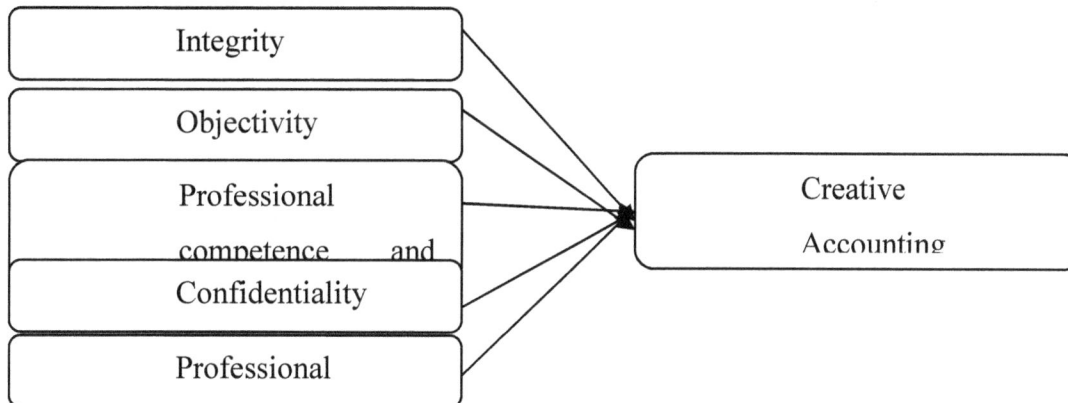

Figure 2.1 Theoretical framework

2.4.1 Hypotheses

Based on the literature and the theoretical framework, the following can be hypothesized:

H1: There is a relationship between integrity and creative accounting practices

H2: There is a relationship between objectivity and creative accounting practices

H3: There is a relationship between professional competence and due care and creative accounting practices

H4: There is a relationship between confidentiality and creative accounting practices

H5: There is a relationship between professional behavior and creative accounting practices.

2.5 Summary

This chapter has presented the literature review of the study. The chapter has discussed the creative accounting practices and their area, techniques, reason to conduct creative accounting practices, and the methods to prevent the creative accounting practices. The chapter as well has reviewed and discussed the ethical commitment and its definitions and relationship with the creative accounting practices. Five elements of the ethical commitments were identified by IFAC. These elements were discussed and reviewed. Based on the literature review, the study has proposed the theoretical framework and its related hypotheses. Five hypotheses that linked the independent variables of this study to the creative accounting practices in Malaysia were proposed.

RESEARCH METHODOLOGY

3.0 Introduction

This chapter is devoted to draw the methodology of this research. It was found that studies related to ethical commitment and its influence on creative accounting are few. This chapter fulfills the objectives of this study by adapting a questionnaire to answer the research questions. The population of the study is the professional accountant in Malaysia. Sample of the study is chosen randomly. The data will be collected using a questionnaire. It will be analyzed using SPSS version 22.0.

3.1 Research Design

This study is quantitative, it focuses on finding the relationship between the ethical commitment elements, and the creative accounting practices in Malaysia. Based on the literature, the study has developed the theoretical framework. This framework will be tested by using data collected via questionnaire. The hypotheses will be tested and the final framework will be derived.

3.2 Population

The population of the study is the professional accountants in Malaysia. According to Malaysian Institute of Certified Public Accountants (MICPA), there are 1,348 professional accountants working in Malaysian firm. Those accountants will be the target respondents of this study.

3.3 Sampling

According to Saharan and Boogie (2003), the sample of the study consists of 306 respondents. The respondents will be chosen randomly. The process of selecting the sample is presented through the following steps:

3.3.1 Sampling Frame

The information about the population and its counts will be obtained from the Malaysian Institute of Certified Public Accountants (MICPA).

3.3.2 Sampling Design

Sampling design is considered as a design, or a working plan, that specifies the population frame, sample size, sample selection, and estimation method in detail. Objective of the sampling design is to know the characteristic of the population. This study specifically investigates the creative accounting practices in Malaysia. It uses the professional accountant as target respondents.

3.3.3 Sampling Technique

The sample is randomly selected because each accountant has the chance to be selected.

3.3.4 Sampling Size

According to Saharan and Boogie (2003) when the population is, 1348 then the sample size can be 306 respondents. This sample can represent the population effectively and sufficiently. Therefore, the sample of this study consists of 306 respondents.

3.3.5 Unit Analysis

The unit analysis of this study is the professional accountant in Malaysia. They are selected due to the experience and being certified professional accountant.

3.4 Data Collection

The data of this study will be collected using online questionnaire. The questionnaire was adopted from other researchers. The sample size of this study is 306. Therefore, a total of 306 questionnaires will be sent to the respondents via emails. The respondents will be given adequate time to answer the questionnaire. Follow up procedure and reminder will be applied.

3.4.1 Instrument

The data is collected via questionnaire. The questionnaire consists of three parts. First part asks about the general information and background information of the respondents. In the second part, the elements of ethical commitment are asked. Third part asks about the creative accounting practices. The questionnaire was adapted from many sources. Integrity, objectivity, and creative accounting were adapted from Al Mopani (2013). Professional competence and due care, confidentiality, and professional behavior were adapted from IFAC (2013).

A copy of the questionnaire is given in Appendix A.

3.4.2 Pilot Study

Since the instrument is adapted from other researchers, it is important to assess the reliability of the instrument and the understanding of the respondents of the questions. A pilot study will be conducted on 30 master students at IUKL. The response will be checked for reliability and the comments of the respondents will be taken and corrective actions will be made accordingly.

3.5 Data Analysis

The data analysis will be conducted using the Statistical Package for the Social Sciences (SPSS) version 22.0. The findings will be present through descriptive analysis of the background information and variable of the study.

Reliability analysis will be presented to ensure that the measurements are reliable. Lastly, the hypotheses of this study will be tested using a Pearson correlation analysis to identify the relationship between the independent variables and the dependent variable.

3.6 Summary

This chapter has presented the methodology of this research. This research is following quantitative approach. A questionnaire adapted from other research is the instrument of data collection. The population includes the professional accountants in Malaysia. A total of 306 respondents will be the sample of this study. Data analysis will be conducted using SPSS version 22.0.

This study aims to find the impact of ethical commitment elements on the creative accounting practices in Malaysia. Because you are professional accountant and have the experience and knowledge about the topic of this study, you are invited to answer these questions.

I would like to assure to you that your identity and the responses that you give will be kept confidential. No one will be able to view your answers except the researcher.

Please spend ten minutes to answer the questionnaire. I would like to thank you very much for your time and effort.

Your efforts is highly appreciated

Part One: Background Information

Please tick (√) on the given box or fill in the blank what represents your answer.

1- Gender

Male	
Female	

2- Age

Less than 30 years	
30 and less than 40 years	
40 and less than 50 years	
50 and less than 60 years	
60 years and more	

3- Educational Level

Diploma Degree	
Bachelor Degree	
Master Degree	
PhD Degree	
Professional	

4- Year-Experience

Less than 5 years	
5 and less than 10 years	
10 and less than 15 years	
15 and less than 20 years	
20 years and more	

Part Two: Ethical Commitments

Please tick (√) on the given numbers in blank what represents your answer.

1= Strongly Disagree, **2** = Disagree, **3** = either agree or Disagree, **4** = Agree,
5 = Strongly Agree.

Integrity						
	Description					
	I am committed to the integrity in all my works.					
	I perform my professional responsibility with the highest sense of integrity.					
	I am free of conflict of interest while I am performing my work					
	I don't knowingly misrepresent facts or subordinate my judgment to other while I am performing my work					

	Objectivity					
	Description					
	I attempt to be objective while I am practicing my work					
	I attempt to maintain objectivity in all my work					
	I am able to take unbiased viewpoint in the performance of my work					
	I avoid relationships that allow bias or have influence on others to override objectivity.					
	I am free of conflict of interest					

	Professional Competence and Due Care					
	Description					
	I do the professional responsibilities with the utmost care necessary to perform the work.					
	I keep an appropriate level of competence and professionalism by developing my professional skills through training and education.					
	I am trying to solve all the problems and difficulties of the work carefully in accordance to the law.					
	I perform my work in accordance to the professional standards					
	I provide my employer with competent professional service					

	Confidentiality					
	Description					
	I am committed to maintain the confidentiality of information relating to the profession.					
	I never disclose any confidential information about the business.					
	I never disclose any data or information in the financial statements unless there is an authorization to do so.					
	I only disclose the information when it is required by law.					

	Professional Behavior					
	Description					
	I always obey the laws and regulations issued by the legislative bodies of the profession.					
	I always stay away from any outside deviation of the rules of ethical conduct for the profession.					
	I work independently to preserve the honor of the profession.					
	I solve the issues of different opinion according to the rules and behaviors of the profession.					
	I avoid deviations in loyalty between the bosses and the required professional standards of conduct.					

Part Three: Creative Accounting

Please tick (√) on the given numbers in blank what represents your answer.

1= Strongly Disagree, **2** = Disagree, **3** = either agree or Disagree, **4** = Agree, **5** = Strongly Agree.

	Creative Accounting					
	Description					
	The accounting reports are to convey information to investors.					
	The financial report is an effective means by which managers can convey information about their firms.					
	Malaysian investors take audited reports as authentic and signifying the true state of the company's affairs.					
	Most preparers of financial reports avoid engaging in creative accounting.					
	Financial regulators have what it takes to check the practice of creative accounting in Malaysia.					
	As an investor, very unhappy if I discover that the company management has been cooking the books of accounts presented to shareholders.					
	Companies use creative accounting to					

	reduce amount of tax					
	I do not support the practice of creative accounting.					
	Activities of creative accounting have impact on the firm's value.					
	From an ethical angle, creative accounting is not desirable.					

(Department of Accounting, College of Administration and Economics/ University of Basra, Iraq)
hisham noori hussain AL-hashimy   978-1-62265-912-8 (online) 978-1-62265-913-5 (paper)

CHAPTER5

A Review of Factor Influencing Online Customer Satisfaction

Abstract

Online customers' satisfaction is one of the newly emerging variables in the literature. Many studies have been conducted to identify the factors that influence this variable. The purpose of this study is to review the literature and identify the factors that influence online customers' satisfaction. A quantitative approach was employed in this study. Articles related to the topic were identified, reviewed, and analyzed. This study is based on secondary data. The findings literature was categorized into four categories. The findings of the study indicated that there are many constructs that have been used intensively in the literature of online customers' satisfaction. First construct is quality and its dimensions, the second construct is website characteristic, and the third construct is trust. This is followed by ease of use, security and privacy, and price. In addition, the findings showed that almost all the studies have used a quantitative approach where a questionnaire was the instrument of data collection. Recommendations for more qualitative studies and studies in trust and service quality were given.
Keywords: Online Customer Satisfaction, Quality, Website Characteristic, Trust

1.0 Introduction

Since the invention of the internet and its widespread during 1990s, it was possible for an individual to shop online. Number of shopper has increased enormously. This was associated with increase in the activities of online buying and selling. The growth in online business has urged practitioners along with academicians to investigate heavily the online customer

(Department of Accounting, College of Administration and Economics/ University of Basra, Iraq)
hisham noori hussain AL-hashimy   978-1-62265-912-8 (online) 978-1-62265-913-5 (paper)

satisfaction. Researchers indicated that the number of online shoppers has increase to include 27% of the world population (Deal joy website, 2014).

Online customer satisfaction is defined by many researchers. One of the definitions is given by Liu et al (2008) who defined online customer satisfaction as an affective state representing an emotional reaction to the entire online shopping experience. The definition of the authors is focusing on the evaluation process that associated with customers online experiences.

Previous studies have intensively investigated the online customer satisfaction. They have used different models and variables to explain the satisfaction of customers in online environment. The majority of researchers have focused on the characteristic of the website and the quality of the information provided to customers (Lin et al. 2011; Bay et al. 2014; Lin and Sun, 2009). However, the literature lacks for studies that review the factors that influence online customer's satisfaction. This study reviews and integrates the literature to provide a comprehensive view of the factors that influence the online customer's satisfaction.

The study consists of five sections. First section has presented the introduction of the study. In the second section, a summary of literature is presented. Third section presents the research methodology. Fourth section presents the findings of the study. Last section concludes the study and provides recommendation for future work.

(Department of Accounting, College of Administration and Economics/ University of Basra, Iraq)
hisham noori hussain AL-hashimy   978-1-62265-912-8 (online) 978-1-62265-913-5 (paper)

www.ingramcontent.com/pod-product-compliance
Lightning Source LLC
Chambersburg PA
CBHW081535220326
41598CB00036B/6440